DON PATERSON

WRITERS AND THEIR WORK

SERIES EDITORS:

Professor Dinah Birch CBE,
University of Liverpool
Professor Dame Janet Beer,
University of Liverpool

Writers and Their Work, launched in 1994 in association with the British Council, won immediate acclaim for its publication of brief but rigorous critical examinations of the works of distinguished writers and schools of writing. The series embraces the best of modern literary theory and criticism, and features studies of many popular contemporary writers, as well as the canonical figures of literature and important literary genres.

© Copyright 2021 by Ben Wilkinson

First published in 2021 by
Liverpool University Press
4 Cambridge Street
Liverpool L69 7ZU

on behalf of
Northcote House Publishers Ltd
Mary Tavy
Devon PL19 9PY

British Library Cataloguing-in-Publication Data
A catalogue record for this book is available from the British Library

ISBN 978-1-80085-537-3

Typeset by Carnegie Book Production, Lancaster
Printed and bound by CPI Group (UK) Ltd, Croydon CR0 4YY

DON PATERSON

Ben Wilkinson

NORTHCOTE

for Ms Fowler and Mrs Trubshaw

Education is not the filling of a pail,
but the lighting of a fire

Contents

Acknowledgements

Many thanks to Christabel Scaife at Liverpool University Press for her patience during the long road to this book's completion; to Alan Buckley, Niall Campbell, Kayo Chingonyi, Steven Earnshaw, Alan Gillis, Chris Jones, Helen Mort, Conor O'Callaghan, and Maurice Riordan for their advice and/or encouragement at key junctures; and to my good friend Alan Malpass, for many reassuring conversations on the life of the early career researcher.

Thanks to Faber and to Rogers, Coleridge & White for permission to quote from several poems, and to Don Paterson for taking the time to check the factual accuracy of the biographical outline, as well as providing helpful assistance at various stages throughout this book's completion.

The discussion of 'An Elliptical Stylus' in Chapter 1 draws in part from my paper '"Something axiomatic on the nature of articulacy": Don Paterson's "An Elliptical Stylus" as *ars poetica*'. Thanks to Peter Boxall for publishing this article in *Textual Practice* (32:4, 2018).

Thanks are also due to Sheffield Hallam University, the Arts and Humanities Research Council, and the University of Bolton for support that enabled the writing of this book.

Biographical Outline

1963	Born Dundee, Scotland, 30 October.
1979	Leaves school to pursue career in music. Briefly works at DC Thomson comics.
1984	Moves to London. Takes lessons from the guitarist Derek Bailey. Tours and records with Ken Hyder's Talisker, as well as a number of free improvisation groups. Works as peripatetic music teacher.
1985–89	Forms the Celtic-influenced jazz group Lammas with saxophonist Tim Garland. Begins attending regular poetry workshops with other upcoming poets, including Lavinia Greenlaw, Maurice Riordan, Jo Shapcott, and Michael Donaghy. In 1989, moves to Brighton.
1990	Receives Eric Gregory Award from the Society of Authors for poets under the age of thirty.
1992	'An Elliptical Stylus' is awarded third place in The Poetry Society's National Poetry Competition.
1993	*Nil Nil*, his first full-length collection of poems, is published by Faber. It receives excellent reviews and wins the Forward Prize for Best First Collection and a Scottish Arts Council Book Award. Wins the Arvon International Poetry Competition for 'A Private Bottling'.
1994–96	Becomes Creative Writing Fellow at the University of Dundee. Named by The Poetry Society as one of twenty New Generation poets, a promotion highlighting significant voices in contemporary British poetry.

1997	Returns to London. Second collection, *God's Gift to Women*, published by Faber. It is awarded both the Geoffrey Faber Memorial Prize and the T. S. Eliot Prize for Poetry. Begins work as Editor for the Picador Poetry list, a division of Pan Macmillan. Also works as freelance journalist, writing videogame reviews for *The Times* and an arts column for *Scotland on Sunday*.
1999	Moves to Edinburgh. Publishes a third collection with Faber, *The Eyes*, translated versions after Antonio Machado. Edits *101 Sonnets: From Shakespeare to Heaney* (Faber), an anthology of classic, modern, and contemporary sonnets. Birth of twin sons, Jamie and Russell.
2001	Moves from Edinburgh to Kirriemuir, Scotland.
2003	*Landing Light*, a fourth collection with Faber, wins the Whitbread Award for Poetry and an unprecedented second T. S. Eliot Prize. Begins teaching in the School of English at the University of St Andrews.
2004	Publishes first book of aphorisms, *The Book of Shadows* (Picador). Edits *New British Poetry* with Charles Simic, a survey anthology introducing contemporary British poets to an American audience, published by Graywolf Press.
2006	Publishes *Orpheus* with Faber, a translation of Rainer Maria Rilke's *Sonnets to Orpheus*, to positive reviews.
2007	Moves to St Andrews, Scotland. Publishes second book of aphorisms, *The Blind Eye: A Book of Late Advice* (Faber).
2008	Awarded the OBE. 'Love Poem for Natalie "Tusja" Beridze' wins the Forward Prize for Best Single Poem.
2009	*Rain*, a sixth volume, is published by Faber and is awarded the Forward Prize for Best Collection of the Year. The book receives many positive reviews, and is praised in *The Guardian* by the Poet Laureate Carol Ann Duffy as 'the best collection of poetry to appear in years … To read this book is to have the privilege of seeing a world-class talent assert itself.' It is published in an American edition in 2010 by Farrar, Straus and Giroux, and reviewed positively in *The New Yorker*.

2010   Awarded the Queen's Gold Medal for Poetry. *Reading Shakespeare's Sonnets*, a reader's guide, is published by Faber.

2012   Returns to Edinburgh. *Selected Poems* published by Faber.

2014   *Smith: A Reader's Guide to the Poetry of Michael Donaghy*, is published by Picador.

2015   Publishes a seventh book of poems with Faber, *40 Sonnets*, which is awarded the Costa Prize for Poetry. The book is subsequently published in an American edition by Farrar, Straus and Giroux in 2017.

2018   *The Poem: Lyric, Sign, Metre*, a treatise on the art of poetry, published by Faber.

2020   Publishes an eighth book of poems, *Zonal*, with Faber.

Abbreviations

I have used the *Selected Poems* (London: Faber, 2012) where possible, cited in the text as *SP*, followed by a page number. In instances where poems from individual collections and aphorisms from books of aphorisms are cited, the following abbreviations are used:

GG   *God's Gift to Women* (London: Faber, 1997)
LL   *Landing Light* (London: Faber, 2003)
NN   *Nil Nil* (London: Faber, 1993)
O   *Orpheus* (London: Faber, 2006)
R   *Rain* (London: Faber, 2009)
TE   *The Eyes* (London: Faber, 1999)
Z   *Zonal* (London: Faber, 2020)
40S   *40 Sonnets* (London: Faber, 2015)

BE   *The Blind Eye: A Book of Late Advice* (London: Faber, 2007)
TBS   *The Book of Shadows* (London: Picador, 2004)

Prologue

The Scottish author Don Paterson is widely regarded as the leading British poet of his generation. Dynamic, interrogative, and unsettling; crafted yet open-ended; fiercely smart, savage, and stirring – from the get-go, his poetry has made for essential reading. Between them, his eight collections of poetry to date – *Nil Nil* (1993), *God's Gift to Women* (1997), *The Eyes* (1999), *Landing Light* (2003), *Orpheus* (2006), *Rain* (2009), *40 Sonnets* (2015), and *Zonal* (2020) – have won numerous literary prizes. He is the only poet in the history of the T. S. Eliot Prize to win the award twice, he has received the Forward Prize in every category (Best Collection, Best First Collection, and Best Single Poem), and in 2010 he was awarded the Queen's Gold Medal for Poetry. Accolades are not always reliable indicators of lasting literary value, but to garner them in the quantity that Paterson's poetry has, from judging panels that extend beyond the British poetry community to include authors, critics, readers, and cultural commentators, confirms his poetry's broad appeal and significance. As one critic has remarked: 'Ask any reader of British poetry to identify who is doing the best work right now, and you should get short odds on the answer being Don Paterson. In a community increasingly divided ... there is something reassuring about the consensus surrounding Paterson. He emerged in the early 1990s as a key figure, and since then his reputation has only grown.'[1]

As such, his critical stock is beginning to rise: a sixth collection, *Rain*, commanded lengthy reviews in *The New Yorker* and *The Times Literary Supplement*, and essays on his work have appeared in anthologies including *The Edinburgh Companion to Contemporary Scottish Poetry* (2009). In spite of this, no study providing a clear overview of Paterson's oeuvre has, until now, existed. There have been book-length works on his British contemporaries Carol Ann Duffy and Simon Armitage, and, in 2014, *Don Paterson: Contemporary Critical Essays* provided a collection of assorted essays on the poet's work as poet, editor, theorist, and cultural arbiter. But the need for a comprehensive study focused primarily on Paterson's poetry was yet to be addressed. On one level, it was this need that led me to write this book.

But Paterson's poetry also reveals the unusual development of a paradoxically shifting yet singular poetic sensibility. Edna Longley has praised his work for 'taking up the problematic questions of selfhood where Louis MacNeice and Philip Larkin left off';[2] A. S. Byatt has singled out the 'life, energy, verbal precision and inventiveness' of his poems;[3] while Paul Muldoon describes him as 'simply the most interesting mid-career poet at work in the UK'.[4] Muldoon's statement in particular hints at how, compared with that of his contemporaries, Paterson's work has taken a striking trajectory. Rather than looking to achieve originality through the typical refinement of an idiosyncratic poetic voice, each of Paterson's published poetry collections to date represents a stylistic sea change, what Sean O'Brien argues is the result of 'a process of attempted self-cancellation, a shedding of particulars in pursuit of a final adaptability'.[5]

Beneath the stylistic evidence of this process is the deeper sense – evident in both Paterson's poems and his critical prose – of a growing poetic vision. This is best understood as rooted in Paterson's conviction that 'a poet should be in service to the poem, and while that's the case, nothing exists except the poem; the poem annihilates the poet'.[6] It is this belief in the poem as an art form that is self-contained and self-sustaining, creating its own autonomous universe, which often seems to guide his writing. In the unambiguously titled 'Poetry' (one of Paterson's 'versions' after the Spanish of Antonio Machado, collected in his third volume *The Eyes*) the speaker, in a moment of aphoristic revelation, suggests that

> the pure verse, when it finally comes, will sound
> like a mountain spring, anonymous and serene.

As if to dispel any doubts, the sonnet concludes:

> Beneath the blue oblivious sky, the water
> sings of nothing, not your name, not mine. (*SP* 71)

As will be illustrated throughout this study, beyond the marked impact of Machado's *via negativa*,[7] which Paterson applauds as evidence of a poet 'obsessed with the suppression of his own ego' (*TE* 55), the influence of Jorge Luis Borges's philosophical parables and the eerily suspended aphorisms of Antonio Porchia can be seen to bolster this belief in the poem as a self-governing creation, whose success depends on detaching itself from its human source. This aesthetic, defined as much by prose writers and philosophical thinkers in the tradition as it is by poetic forebears, is one where any final approach is precluded. For Paterson, this is in the hope of allowing what might be termed the most poetically true, rather than any diminishingly intended, writing to emerge. 'I do not know which of us has written this page' states Borges's divided narrator,[8] chiming with Porchia's maxim, 'My "I" has gone farther and farther away from me. Today it is my farthest "you".'[9] Alongside scrutiny of the recurrent motifs and the stylistic and thematic features of Paterson's poetry, an understanding of this compositional allegiance to the individual poem enables the most rewarding readings of Paterson's work.

However, Paterson's poetic practice is not merely an updated version of the Modernist aesthetic of T. S. Eliot and Ezra Pound. This study will discuss how his work shares affinities with Eliot's influential statement in 'Tradition and the Individual Talent', in which he claims that 'the progress of an artist is a continual self-sacrifice, a continual extinction of personality'.[10] But I will also show how the poems move beyond Eliot's willed workshopping of the poetic self, uncovering the ways in which the poems adhere too closely to direct address of the reader to fit fully with Eliot's sense of a 'process of depersonalisation', in which the art of poetry 'may be said to approach the condition of science'.[11]

Paterson's defining view of the successful poem as an autonomous creation, however, remains central to his poetry. With its playful assertion that there is 'no I to speak of', 'A

Talking Book' (*LL* 27) from Paterson's fourth collection, *Landing Light*, overtly reiterates the earlier mantra of 'Poetry', while one of Paterson's most repeated poetic claims maintains that 'a poem is a little machine for remembering itself'.[12] Here, the suggestion is that our memory of the poem *is* the poem itself, belonging to the reader as much as its author. But the 'impersonality' of Paterson's verse must always be considered alongside the emotionally direct, witty, and entertaining address it often strikes, as well as the sometimes confessional and consistent nature of the personae that are variously deployed in his writing.

What further separates Paterson from the Modernist aesthetic are his specific misgivings about contemporary poetry, and his unfashionable conviction that writing poems can still be a moral project. Speaking about poetry's current position as a 'marginal art form', he has argued that 'one of the legacies of Modernism is that somehow we poets managed to make ourselves irrelevant to a general readership that had instinctively come to poetry for, and it sounds heretical to say this, moral education and comfort'.[13] In the aforementioned 'A Talking Book', ambition may be veiled by the poem's playful narrative tone, but the declaration of poetry's power to impart knowledge and real feeling cannot be ignored. While the two may not appear immediately connected, this concern about poets – and, by extension, poems – losing the conviction and authority they once possessed, 'until they say so little that no one wants to listen to them at all',[14] is closely bound with the belief that a good poem should sing alone. Rarely one to mince his words, Paterson is clearly opposed to a trend he identifies as exhibiting a panicked 'fear of boring the reader', with every line having 'three interesting things in it because the poet is terrified of the reader falling asleep'.[15] We need only look to his *ars poetica*, particularly his major work of poetic theory *The Poem: Lyric, Sign, Metre* (2018), to find the claim that 'the good poem often seems to arrive with an air of perfect inevitability'.[16] Paterson takes issue with 'academic accounts' of verse and what he sees as their confusion between 'intrinsic technique' and 'extrinsic effect', bolstering his view of good poetry as a spell-like, self-affirming creation that, in entering the collective unconscious through virtue of its memorability, has the power to alter the way we view the world.[17] As Paterson claims, 'poetry emerges naturally from our speech as the immediate consequence of emotional urgency, and our desire to communicate this urgency by organising ... those natural features of language that best carry it'.[18]

Alongside these concepts of what poetry is, and what purpose it can (and perhaps should) be put, is what we might call the philosophical hinterland to Paterson's poems. A recurring quotation in Paterson's critical writings is Charles Simic's remark that poems are 'translations from the silence'.[19] For Paterson, this silence is much more than the empty air into which the notes of the Orphic lyre are played. It also embodies what his poems frequently pose as the false divide between the 'real' and the symbolic, or more specifically 'the human dream' we inhabit, an all-pervasive trap our consciousnesses fall prey to, in which the labelling-gun of language, as Paterson has it, makes 'everything appear purely in the guise of its human utility, and held in place by its human name' (*TBS* 13). Part of poetry's moral purpose, in Paterson's view, often seems to be in acting as a kind of temporary corrective to our perceptually restrictive state of consciousness, serving to open the doors of perception in making valuable additions to our stock of available reality. In Paterson's sixth collection of poems, *Rain*, the vignette 'The Error' provides a précis of this existential dilemma:

> As the bird is to the air
> and the whale is to the sea
> so man is to his dream.
>
> His world is just the glare
> of the world's utility
> returned by his eye-beam.
>
> Each self-reflecting mind
> is in this manner destined
> to forget its element,
>
> and this is why we find
> however deep we listen
> that the skies are silent. (*SP* 140)

Given that the metaphysical implications of 'the human dream' have come to dominate Paterson's thinking, any reading of his oeuvre must consider its profound influence on the poetry. But it is also worth noting that such concerns are subtly present in a number of his early poems, where shifts between everyday false distinctions expose reductive thinking to the almost ungraspable complexity of truths lurking beneath our perceptions. We might often like to think of art as mirroring life, acting as mere copy of reality's truths, but Paterson's poems are keen to show that, at best, the 'real' can be seen as a fundamentally unknowable realm beyond our blinkered human perceptions, and, at worst, a flimsy construct shored up by the ignorance of uninterrogated anthropocentrism.

Beyond the philosophical concerns that undoubtedly inform the poems, however, any account of Paterson's poetry, as Alan Gillis notes, 'will be incomplete if it does not allow for his vim and unpredictable energy, his fresh-air inventiveness and wit'.[20] Nor will any critical engagement succeed if it overlooks the connected verisimilitude of his work, borne of a talent for drawing the mythical and spiritual from out of the quotidian – a feature that often lends the poems their surface effervescence. Paterson's poems are as much engaged with the abstract, philosophical, and hallucinatory as they are with the life-as-lived world of sport, sex, drink, music, class politics, and, in his later writing, fatherhood, middle age, friendship, grief, and loss. In fact, their power often lies in recognising that distinctions between ordinariness and otherness swiftly collapse under interrogative lyric enquiry.

The shifting yet cohesive nature of Paterson's verse requires a reader to recognise its dualities. These include – though as we shall see, are by no means confined to – an individual, sometimes deceptively autobiographical poetic voice as played against conflicting personae, unreliable narrators, and a recurrent obsession with the instability and unknowability of the self; an allegiance to the lyric tradition, forms, and the musical craft of poetry as challenged by frequent stylistic fractures, contorted sequences, and the foregrounding of postmodern play; and a strikingly modern, philosophical, often amused and sceptical engagement with the world, while also maintaining a partly religious sense of wonder in its existential concerns. These are expressed in tones that are by turns direct, colloquial, eloquent, playful, and profoundly philosophical. Allowing for the free play of these competing features will, I hope, assist readers in the fullest appreciation of Paterson's poems.

Paterson's aesthetic might be best understood as one dominated by seeming paradox and contradiction. Here is a poet fundamentally concerned with 'the age-old task of making the normal and habitual appear newly strange'.[21] One could pick almost any poem from his oeuvre and find that the surreal and the mystical are never far removed from the rooted detail of the quotidian. In this way, paradox and contradiction supply the intellectual means by which Paterson addresses the core thematic concern of his work: the divide between our routine encounters with the world, and the sense that the complex nature of reality lies beyond the perceptually restricted state of human consciousness. As Sean O'Brien has written, 'Paterson's poems reveal a determination to use poetry as a kind of thinking, rather than be the passive prisoner of period and style and received ideas.'[22] In this sense, his work bears out the concept of defamiliarisation, proposed by the Russian formalist Victor Shklovsky in his essay 'Art as Technique':

> The purpose of art is to impart the sensation of things as they are perceived and not as they are known. The technique of art is to make objects 'unfamiliar', to make forms difficult, to increase the difficulty and length of perception because the process of perception is an aesthetic end in itself and must be prolonged. *Art is a way of experiencing the artfulness of an object: the object is not important.*[23]

The key stylistic features of Paterson's poetry – the deft use of quotidian detail, the idiomatic assurance of direct address to the reader, and the increased anonymity of poetic voice catalysed by experimental use of personae – can all be seen as facilitators to the interrogative philosophical thinking and imaginative transformation that the poems insist upon. Though a poet's theoretical pronouncements and their actual poetic practice do not map precisely onto one another, it is revealing that Paterson argues for poetry's transformative responsibility in much of his *ars poetica*. A notable example is in 'The Dark Art of Poetry', his T. S. Eliot lecture of 2004. Having criticised the 'populist' strand of mainstream poetry that trades in 'recognition comedy' (which, according to Paterson, demonstrates 'no need either for originality or epiphany', merely portraying things in the habitual manner to which we are accustomed to perceiving them), as well as avant-garde tendencies that he diagnoses as 'so desperate for transcendence they see it everywhere', Paterson expounds on what he views to be those 'risks' taken by the best poems:

> Risk, of the sort that makes readers feel genuinely uncomfortable, excited, open to suggestion, vulnerable to reprogramming, complicit in the creative business of their transformation – is quite different. Real danger flirts with the things we most dread as poets. Perhaps the biggest risk of all is that of being largely understood and then found to be talking a pile of garbage. But risk is also writing with real feeling, as Frost did, while somehow avoiding sentimentality; simplicity, as Cavafy did, and somehow avoiding artlessness; daring to be prophetic, as Rilke did, and miraculously avoiding pretentiousness; writing with real originality, as Dickinson did, while somehow avoiding cliché ... The narrowest of these paths, though, the poets' beautiful tightrope-walk, is the one between sense and mystery – to make one, while revealing the other.[24]

This belief that the most rewarding balance a poem can strike is one between sense and mystery is a central feature of Paterson's poetry. Indeed, at about the time of this T. S. Eliot lecture, Paterson briefly occupied a central position within an ongoing controversy in contemporary British poetry. In suggesting that the so-called 'mainstream' (a term with 'vanilla overtones' that might nevertheless usefully describe lyric poets who seek to intelligently engage 'a general – i.e., non-practising and non-academic – readership') occupied the middle ground between the 'infantilising' populists on one side and 'the Postmoderns' on the other (specifically those 'experimental' poets most readily associated with the Cambridge School in the wake of J. H. Prynne), his position was seen as openly antagonistic.[25] Unsurprisingly, Paterson inspired especial ire from the Cambridge School when he further proposed that their collective project was 'unethical', namely for its deliberate use of obfuscating language 'likely to confound the reader'. In mocking fashion, Paterson went on to conclude that such poets 'probably do deserve to inherit the earth, being the first literary movement to have conceived the masterstroke of eliminating the reader entirely'.[26]

Though Paterson has since taken a much more placative position, with such tribalism in contemporary British poetry having significantly waned, his specific sense of poetry's clarifying moral project remains. As we shall see in close readings of the work, Paterson's arsenal of poetic techniques is deployed as a means of interrogating received ideas and assumptions, though he seeks to achieve this through a poetry of plain sense, altering the reader's perceptions through exposing the intrinsic otherness of the apparently ordinary. This is not to suggest that Paterson's poetry, in John Keats's rightly disparaging sense, 'has a palpable design upon us'.[27] Not only would this be to ignore the unforced manner in which his poems frequently destabilise and transform their quotidian settings, it would also discount the autonomous qualities of his poems. As Paterson himself has stated: 'As soon as you start thinking about the audience, if you start second guessing what the audience might like, then you're lost; all you should ever be thinking about is the poem.'[28] Rather, in Paterson's poems 'the structure is as important as the fracture; one cannot exist without the other'.[29] One way in which this can be understood is how the poems' increasing clarity of syntax and pared-back diction deliver the 'structure' of plain sense so as to enable the subtle 'fracture' of their subject matter. As O'Brien states: 'At the same time as Paterson's own work undertakes an increasingly strict rationing of "personality", his metaphysical cast of mind and imagination leads to a much firmer assertion that poetry is a mode of knowledge than perhaps we are accustomed to.'[30]

Reading Paterson's work, as with that of many of our best poets, you become especially aware that unexpected truths can often be revealed in poetry through the dramatised merging of quotidian ordinariness and supernatural otherness. This approach is one that necessarily requires a degree of exaggerative imaginativeness and invention. The imaginative world, after all, has its own veracity: in seeking not to offer absolute truths, but intuitive ones that can often seem truer than the simple sense data or qualia we glean from the physical world, poetry can be seen to distinguish itself from other forms of intellectual enquiry. As Paterson has recommended: 'Every morning the writer should go to the window, look out and remind himself of this fact: aside from his own species, not one thing he sees – not one bird, tree or stone – has in its possession the name he gives it' (*TBS* 136). An allegiance to poetic truth, as Paterson's poetry evinces, is not then a persistent attempt to 'accurately' describe, but rather a destabilisation of conventional representations and an interrogation of received ideas so as to deliver a transformative payoff, altering the reader's preconceived perceptions. In this way, poetry becomes a mode of knowledge, a means of making greater sense of the world.

As already suggested, Paterson's poetry to date has followed a marked stylistic trajectory, while also maintaining a thematic consistency. Revealing an abiding interest in their underpinning thematic concern – the divide between our routine encounters with the world, and the sense that the complex nature of reality lies beyond the perceptually restricted state of human consciousness – his poems' explorations have deepened as Paterson's concept of poetry as a mode of knowledge has come to the fore. Suffice to say for now, as cautious as these explorations manifest themselves in his first volume, *Nil Nil*, they lay the groundwork for Paterson's later work, and its increasing dedication to poetry as a mode of knowledge. As Patrick Crotty noted of second collection *God's Gift to Women*: 'The high jinks about trains and the naming and fate of defunct Dundee stations ... like the volume's general air of knowing cleverness, could not quite hide the unusual scale and seriousness of the poet's agitation by "big" questions of religion and sexuality.'[31] With the consequent translation project of third collection *The Eyes*, Paterson's poetry can be seen to have granted itself greater scope to explore these philosophical proclivities. These translated 'versions' of the poems of Antonio Machado capture, as Michael Wood has said, 'a peculiar aptitude for reflecting on poems while writing them, and for making the poet not a forlorn artist or a suffering everyman, and not even, essentially, a projection of the historical person of the poet, but the agent of a lyrical intelligence'.[32]

Up to and including the catalytic Machado 'versions' of *The Eyes*, there is a crystallising sense of Paterson's poems developing a philosophical model with which to examine their subject matters. So it is in *Landing Light* (2003) that Paterson's concept of 'the human dream' first overtly appears, issued from the anonymous voice of 'A Talking Book':

By all means, turn the page or close the book.
But first, imagine how this world would look
were it not duly filtered, cropped and strained
into that pinhole camera you call a brain
by whose inverted dim imaginings
you presume to question it. So many things
are hidden from you. Luckily. Here's one. (*LL* 30)

The poem's ludic yet forceful argument runs parallel to the philosophical observations apparent in several of Paterson's aphorisms. 'We live in a human dream', states Paterson in *The Book of Shadows*, 'being one in which everything appears purely in the guise of its human utility, and held in place by its human name. Names are small and sinister metaphors that restrict, absolutely, the use of an object. Our eyes open to this madness every morning; at night we dream within the dream' (*TBS* 13). With *Orpheus*, Paterson's translated 'versions' of Rainer Maria Rilke's *Die Sonette an Orpheus* (1922), the concept of 'the human dream' becomes the encompassing principle of the translation project, foregrounding the philosophical questing and existential musings at the sonnets' cores: 'But is that true?' (*O* 13), 'What was real in that All?' (*O* 38), 'O, where are we now?' (*O* 56). The concept receives further explication in the accompanying 'Afterword', in which the potential fallout of such a hallucinatory state is explored. 'Eventually', writes Paterson, 'the dream becomes so heavily constructed and all-pervasive that we begin to mistake it for our element. We are then in danger of blithely or accidentally destroying our *real* element and habitat, with which we no longer feel any physical continuity' (*O* 71).

The overall impression here – which, as we will discover, the poems of Paterson's sixth collection, *Rain*, most distinctly bear out – is of an ontological attempt to utilise poetry as a means of constructing a worldview. The poetry seeks to combine an objective and godless scientific materialism with the mystery accommodated by a more openly spiritual attitude. Just as Robert Crawford has commented how Paterson's poems can seem like those of one who has 'never forgiven his God for walking out',[33] Sean O'Brien has noted that 'Paterson fell away from Pentecostalism while seeming to take with him an appetite for totalizing depictions of human experience'.[34] The development of Paterson's poetry towards this apparent attempt to uncover an all-encompassing ontology is fascinating, precisely for the way it combines empirical philosophy with spiritual receptivity. This strongly recalls the theoretical writings of the French Symbolist Stéphane Mallarmé, a clear influence on the poet: 'we are merely empty forms of matter', Mallarmé once claimed, 'but we are indeed sublime in having invented God and our soul'.[35] The sense of an underpinning philosophy in Paterson's work holds interesting consequences, in the manner in which it has increasingly shaped the poems' intellectual handling of recurrent subject matter – doubles and doubling, the self, sexuality, death, love, and paternity, among others – but also the way in which it is enacted through the stylistic strategies of the poems.

In a review of *Rain*, Dan Chiasson notes the manner in which a number of that book's elegiac poems exhibit a 'loss-consciousness' that 'changes the meaning of their formalism'.[36] Alongside discussion of Paterson's use of quotidian detail, direct address to the reader, and the adaptable use of poetic voice in several key poems, this study will also explore how Paterson's use of form has become increasingly indispensable to the generation of his poems' metaphysical arguments. As such, it is my hope that this volume will help readers both new to and already familiar with Paterson's poems, to appreciate the imaginative, structural, and stylistic means by which they operate, offering insights into the poems' literary and theoretical forebears and their philosophical hinterland along the way. In doing so, this study will make the case for Paterson as a major lyric poet, assessing how his poems achieve their memorability, emotional and intellectual depths, and remarkable transformative power, in their increasing allegiance to poetry as a mode of knowledge.

1

For the Hell of It: *Nil Nil* (1993)

Whether they intend it or not, the first poem of a poet's first collection will often be read as a statement of intent or *ars poetica*. It is worthwhile beginning with a detailed discussion of 'The Ferryman's Arms', the opening poem in *Nil Nil*, not least because it offers a pertinent illustration of some of the main features of Paterson's early work. Poet-critic Alan Gillis has summarised these as threefold: the poem's use of 'grounded context, detail and atmosphere' to conjure a quotidian setting that is, in turn, 'pierced through' so as to 'explore underlying black-and-white binaries';[1] its 'open-ended ambiguity that ensures there can be no clear-cut moral distinction' between the realms of the 'real' and the symbolic; and its 'revelation of a bifurcation', particularly within the notion of the self.[2] 'The Ferryman's Arms' begins with an everyday scene, in which the speaker, waiting to catch a boat, decides to pass the time with recreation:

> About to sit down with my half-pint of Guinness
> I was magnetized by a remote phosphorescence
> and drawn, like a moth, to the darkened back room
> where a pool-table hummed to itself in the corner.
> With ten minutes to kill and the whole place deserted
> I took myself on for the hell of it. Slotting
> a coin in the tongue, I looked round for a cue –
> while I stood with my back turned, the balls were deposited
> with an abrupt intestinal rumble; a striplight
> batted awake in its dusty green cowl. (*SP* 3)

At first glance, these lines depict an ordinary setting, but a closer read reveals how the poem is already haunted by a

13

sense of menacing otherness. Note the pool-table that 'hummed to itself' and the coin slotted into its tongue, suggesting the ancient Greek custom of placing the ferryman Charon's fee in the mouths of the deceased, payment for the journey across the River Styx, from the land of the living to the land of the dead. We are reminded of Louis MacNeice's 'Charon', a poem in which a journey that similarly recalls Dante's *Inferno* finds a ferryman transformed: 'He looked at us coldly / And his eyes were dead and his hands on the oar / Were black with obols'.[3] Consequently the speaker, and by extension the reader, senses that they are about to embark on such a voyage, but 'The Ferryman's Arms' more than gestures towards the emergence of this shadowy symbolic realm from within its everyday setting. For one, the speaker talks of having 'ten minutes to kill' when, as William Matthews once memorably noted, it is time that kills us.[4] Moreover, like the pool table, the mundane striplight is seen to have 'batted awake' and appears to be alive. This is more disturbing, since its 'dusty green cowl' conjures the symbolic living embodiment of death, the Grim Reaper, now staring down at the poem's speaker and the game about to commence. In the middle of these two paradoxes – the speaker 'killing' time that is in fact killing him, and the poem's sense that death has come to life – comes the poem's key line, 'I took myself on for the hell of it' (*SP* 3). Here is another paradox: the colloquial term 'for the hell of it' might mean to do something for no reason other than fun or pleasure, but the phrase takes on a more pertinently sinister resonance, given the seemingly literal Hell the speaker appears to be about to experience.

Paradox and contradiction can be seen to supply the intellectual means by which Paterson often addresses the underpinning thematic concern of his work: the divide between our routine encounters with the world, and the sense that the complex nature of reality lies beyond the perceptually restricted state of human consciousness. With this in mind, the aforementioned paradoxes in 'The Ferryman's Arms' suggest more than just the 'revelation of a bifurcation, a split between realms'.[5] In his game of pool against himself, the speaker goes on to 'make an immaculate clearance', telling how 'the black / did the vanishing trick while the white stopped / before gently rolling back as if nothing had happened' (*SP* 3). Here, the ordinary detail of the black-and-white pool balls makes them seem separate and distinct. Yet, by the end of the poem, the speaker boards the ferry and leaves the losing version of himself at the table, 'stuck in his tent of light'.

On the one hand, the black ball can be seen to represent the victorious speaker, 'vanishing' aboard a boat soon to travel across Styx-like waters that are 'as black as my stout', while similarly the white ball represents the losing doppelgänger, who fails to comprehend that the poem's everyday setting is already 'a kind of death-realm'.[6] But, on the other, in spite of its haunting imagery, the world the poem conjures remains rooted in the quotidian, emphasising the fact that winner and loser are still fundamentally one and the same. Black and white, darkness and light, suffering and pleasure, even death and life – the poem suggests that such oppositions not only overlap and blur with one another, but are essentially identical. To understand the complex nature of the human condition, the poem suggests, we must recognise the monistic state of the universe, a 'oneness' that language's attempts to divide and compartmentalise, and the subsequent habitual reality we inhabit, have obscured from view. The resulting implication is that we must also acknowledge the constructed and shifting nature of the self. 'Perhaps, ultimately', Paterson has argued, 'the price of the imaginative life is the knowledge that there is no locus, no centre to which we can hold' (*TBS* 151). As such, 'The Ferryman's Arms' recalls 'The Other' by Edward Thomas, a poem that also addresses a doppelgänger and the sense of a divided, incoherent identity, the understanding of which gives rise to the fruitless pursuit of a 'true' or ideal self. As the speaker in 'The Other' confesses: 'I travelled fast, in hopes I should / Outrun that other. What to do / When caught, I planned not. I pursued / To prove the likeness, and, if true, / To watch until myself I knew.'[7]

'The Ferryman's Arms' may not offer an answer to Thomas's conundrum, but it does supply a kind of coping strategy in its final twist. If we are to make sense of the difficult knowledge that the imaginative life can bring, specifically its manifestation in the writing and close reading of poems, this 'thought has to be dismissed, and dismissed again' (*TBS* 151). To an extent, speaker and reader must act like the white ball on the pool table, 'as if nothing had happened', unless, like the 'foaming lip' of waves on the coast, we want to find ourselves 'trying, with a nutter's persistence, to read / and re-read the shoreline'. The speaker may take himself on 'for the hell of it', dividing black-and-white binaries so as to deconstruct both his unified sense of self and the everyday world around him, but he also returns to a singular concept of himself when boarding the boat, in order to make sense of the experience. 'I got aboard early, / remembering the ferry would leave on the hour / even for only my losing opponent', states the poet, 'but I left him there, stuck in his tent of light'.

In this manner, the opening poem of Paterson's first collection reveals how his poetry's subtle cultivation of paradox, drawn from the everyday details of the quotidian, enables a perceptual transformation. But equally, it intuits the necessity of partly re-subscribing to the habitual reality from which the poem allows a brief departure. Hence Paterson's commitment throughout *Nil Nil* to the solid foundations of the everyday. The poem's suggestion is that, having gleaned this knowledge, we can return to our ordinary lives wiser and, in a sense familiar from the painfully self-aware poetry of Philip Larkin, less deceived. Like Larkin, Paterson's work is concerned with the complex truths that underpin seemingly mundane interactions between individual and world, but his poetics insists on a more enquiring and metaphysical engagement with the fundamental nature of the reality we inhabit. 'The Ferryman's Arms' is therefore not only remarkable for its intense scrutiny of everyday life, enabling poet and reader to reassess uninterrogated assumptions and preconceptions. It also hints at the beginnings of Paterson's broader ontological attempt to utilise poetry as a means of developing a worldview.

Paterson's estrangement of the everyday in the poems of *Nil Nil* can serve to defamiliarise and so allow for an interrogation of unexamined preconceptions and perspectives, but also to destabilise notions of a unified sense of self. W. B. Yeats once claimed that 'we make out of the quarrel with others, rhetoric, but of the quarrel with ourselves, poetry', to which a number of Paterson's poems offer an unusually precise illustration.[8] Several feature speakers who are either morbidly aware of a perceived Cartesian divide between the life of the mind and the life of the flesh, or else of the conflicting, sometimes incompatible facets of their mutable identities.

The former concern is addressed in 'Morning Prayer', Paterson's reworking of 'Oraison du soir' ('Evening Prayer'), by Arthur Rimbaud. Rimbaud's poetry espouses the literary and philosophical aesthetic of those nineteenth-century poets in the lineage of Charles Baudelaire, poets whose collective influence exerts a notable effect on Paterson's early poetry. It is therefore not surprising to find a 'version' of Rimbaud in *Nil Nil*. As the French-language poet Jean Moréas broadly claimed for the Symbolist movement in *The Symbolist Manifesto*: 'in this art, scenes from nature, human activities, and all other real world phenomena will not be described for their own sake; here, they are perceptible surfaces created to represent their esoteric affinities with the primordial ideals'.[9] With their commitment to exposing the complex, elemental otherness lurking within the apparently ordinary, the poems of *Nil Nil* share obvious affinities with this Symbolist poetics. Yet, in loosely translating Rimbaud, Paterson pushes his poem into surprising territory.

'Morning Prayer' replaces the intoxicated night café setting of the original with the hungover morning-after. We find the speaker staring at his reflection:

> I spend my life sitting, like an angel at the barber's,
> with a mug in one hand, fag in the other,
> my froth-slabbered face in the gantry mirror
> while the smoke towels me down, warm and white. (*SP* 4)

Whereas the speaker in 'The Ferryman's Arms' is divided, here he seems reassuringly cohesive. But any comfortable, unified sense of self is short-lived. The optimistic if absurd simile in the speaker's description of himself as 'an angel at the barber's' quickly gives way to the cigarette and morning drink of tea or coffee in either hand, already at odds with one another. As a stimulant, the latter suggests an attempt to revive a hazy and sluggish mindset, but the former provides the opposite, a smokescreen that allows a level of comfort, 'warm and white', in momentarily preventing a clear-eyed analysis of the situation. When the smoke clears, the speaker cannot help but recognise how his bodily impulses tell a truth at odds with his ideal sense of self. He recalls 'old dreams' that barely 'hold their heat' now his heart 'saps itself' and 'stews in its own juice'; he confesses to drinking to excess the night before so as to 'stomach' his worst thoughts; and, by the end of the poem, he seems to resent being trapped in what feels like an alien body, only stirring into life at 'the most bitter necessities' (*SP* 4). If the self can only remain active and practical in maintaining a rootedness to a specific body, as Timothy Donnelly notes, Paterson's poem 'confronts the possibility that … embodiedness itself becomes, at times, indistinguishable from a custodianship to the mechanical exigencies of a material contraption'.[10]

Yet the most surprising aspect of the poem is the way in which it frames this knowledge. In Rimbaud's original, it is the speaker's night-time drunkenness that facilitates his maudlin self-analysis; however true his observations, there is the sense that he will sober up, and so return to an integrated sense of self. In Paterson's poem, however, the same thoughts occur in the context of the morning after drinking. There may be a residual level of intoxication, but it appears that the more the speaker sobers, the more his sense of an irrevocable divide between mind and body takes hold. Unlike Rimbaud's original, which articulates an intoxicated hopelessness, the speaker in 'Morning Prayer' returns to sobriety and supposed normality with these thoughts, lending them the force of a dawning epiphany. However tentatively and obliquely, the poem again marks the beginnings of Paterson's sense of the truth-seeking and transformative possibilities of poetry.

While 'Morning Prayer' exhibits a fascinated disgust with the divide between mind and body, another poem in *Nil Nil*, 'An Elliptical Stylus', addresses the mutability of personal identity, though the effect is similarly one of perceptual transformation. Principally, the poem is a barbed critique of rigid conceptions of social class; it seems to argue that these views remain residually present in late twentieth-century British society, despite an ostensibly increased level of social mobility. Such is the complexity of the poem's repeated volte-face and tonal variance, however, it has elicited an array of critical responses. 'A grabbing of the individual reader by the collar';[11] 'an attack on middle England's complacency';[12] a poem that 'gives us a voice which arrestingly declaims its otherness'[13] while also declaring 'chips on shoulders':[14] these are just a handful of reactions to 'An

Elliptical Stylus'. All of these critics agree on the poem's central theme: as Adam Thorpe summarises, the piece is ostensibly a 'sad little story about the speaker's Scottish working-class father being mocked by a salesman'.[15] But there is much more to 'An Elliptical Stylus' than a tale of masculine pride and posturing.

The initial setting in 'An Elliptical Stylus' is the speaker's uncle's house, where father and speaker-son are given a proud demonstration of the eponymous stylus, a superior needle that enhances the sound quality of a vinyl record player. The poem sets up a conventional dynamic: while the speaker's father is portrayed as voicing his approval with a stereotypically working-class, Scots-inflected tone ('"Aye, yer elliptical stylus – / fairly brings out a' the wee details"'), the speaker recalls the experience with atmospheric, almost florid, descriptive finesse:

> Balanced at a fraction of an ounce
> the fat cartridge sank down like a feather;
> music billowed into three dimensions
> as if we could have walked between the players. (*SP* 10)

The immediate precursor here is Seamus Heaney's 'Digging', the opening poem of his debut collection, *Death of a Naturalist* (1966). Both poems find the articulate poet-son remembering his non-literary father in an attempt to find common ground and continuity between their generational, educational, and vocational differences. The difference between the poems, however, is that where the narrator of 'Digging', despite his admiration, finds he's 'no spade to follow men' like his labouring father, resolving instead to 'dig' with his pen, Paterson's poem sees father and poet-son sharing in an artistic experience.[16] As Sarah Broom notes: 'the father hears the quality of sound produced by the elliptical stylus … and wants to buy one for "our ancient, beat-up Phillips turntable"'.[17] The implication is that, rather than the distant and anonymous father figure in Heaney's 'Digging', present only as 'a clean rasping sound',[18] the poet's father in 'An Elliptical Stylus' is of a certain sophis-tication, someone who can 'appreciate the difference'. Instead of Heaney's fiercely individual image of the 'squat pen', then, which remains a symbol of his solitary artistic seriousness in spite of attempts to metaphorically connect that object to his father's spade, Paterson's deployment of the stylus, of 'music billowing into three dimensions', evinces a collective aesthetic appreciation. It suggests that the poem's overt focus will not be a class divide between father and son, but the broader class anxieties that the speaker not only recalls from childhood, but also finds apparent in his later adult life.

The poem's second stanza sees father and son arrive at the shop. Met with condescension from the owner given the obvious age of their record player, the poet-narrator recalls how 'we had the guy in stitches: "You can't ... / er ... you'll have to *upgrade your equipment*."' The stanza's pathos is palpable: the speaker notes how the middle-class owner 'sent us from the shop', implying a clear social hierarchy, while the box of needles they end up with are 'thick as carpet-tacks, / the only sort they made to fit our model' (*SP* 10). This descriptiveness sets the scene and supplies the emotional resonance that draws the reader into the poem. The part-jokey, part-dejected tone also makes the sudden, disorienting turn that follows – a characteristic feature of Paterson's writing – all the more effective and jolting.

This third stanza sees the poet-narrator invite the reader to 'eavesdrop' on the poem he instead might be writing, were he the shop owner's son. The parody is sharply executed:

> (Supposing I'd been *his* son: let's eavesdrop
> on 'Fidelities', the poem I'm writing now:
> *The day my father died, he showed me how*
> *he'd prime the deck for optimum performance:*
> *it's that lesson I recall – how he'd refine*
> *the arm's weight, to leave the stylus balanced*
> *somewhere between ellipsis and precision,*
> *as I gently lower the sharp nib to the line*
> *and wait for it to pick up the vibration*
> *till it moves across the page, like a cardiograph ...*) (*SP* 10)

Several critics have explored this 'striking ... parenthetical stanza',[19] finding in its delicate and controlled nostalgia a clear send-up of the perceived qualities of middle-class verse: 'restraint, precision, clarity, balance'.[20] There is also a disruption of preconceptions, as the poet-speaker, having previously asserted his working-class credentials, subverts them (and any easy judgements) in a falsely empathetic, barbed, yet accomplished description of middle-class inheritance. The title of this 'alternative' poem is immediately telling. In its witty punning on the superior quality of sound the elliptical stylus produces, 'Fidelities' not only gestures towards that which father and son have been denied, but also serves to mock naïve notions of poetry as a means of capturing 'true' feeling and meaning through apparently faithful representations of a reified conception of actuality. The poem's delicious lampoon of such an approach – 'lowering the sharp nib to the line', as if the stylus (but also the poet's pen) might 'pick up the vibration' of authentic feeling 'till it moves across the page, like a cardiograph' – is thus a subtle refusal of documentary truth, in favour of what might be termed poetic truth. As outlined, rather than a persistent attempt to 'accurately' describe, in these terms, Paterson sees poetry as characterised by its interrogation of conventional representations and ideas, so as to deliver a transformative payoff that alters our preconceptions.

Given this intricate web of ideas lurking behind the poem's surface play, it is worth considering the way in which the poem's parenthetical stanza not only posits but actually creates a parallel universe, reminiscent of those in a number of the short stories of Jorge Luis Borges. After all, 'Fidelities', like 'An Elliptical Stylus', is pointedly introduced as 'the poem *I'm writing now*'. In interview, Paterson has commented how 'Borges is just as big an influence, possibly more of an influence, than any poet' on his work and, indeed, 'An Elliptical Stylus' is one of several poems in *Nil Nil* that combines the quotidian with a labyrinthine Borgesian conceit to startling effect.[21] The conceit recalls the divided self of 'Borges and I', in which the narrator becomes aware of the disorienting dual life he leads as both author and individual. In Borges's story, a first-person voice narrates, but its identity is divided, between one that inhabits the suspended medium of language, and another that lives an everyday life, unavoidably detached from the former's literary creations. Yet, as the story implies, while author and individual may not be identical, neither are they, as facets of the one person, fully separate or distinct. As the narrator states, it is impossible to know 'which of us has written this page'.[22]

In this sense, 'An Elliptical Stylus' can be seen to interrogate the distinction between the real and the symbolic, or, more specifically, to shake us from 'the human dream'. This is

Paterson's Heideggerian coinage for what he views as the perceptually limited human condition, whereby the labelling-gun of language makes 'everything appear purely in the guise of its human utility, and held in place by its human name' (*TBS* 13). As we will see, the philosophical implications of 'the human dream' come to dominate Paterson's later work. But it is also worth noting that a fascination with the deceptions of routinely perceived reality are present in an early poem such as 'An Elliptical Stylus'. In reading the parenthetical excerpt from 'Fidelities' less as an imaginary flight of fancy, and more as a poem by another poet who, inhabiting a possible parallel universe, is selfsame to the speaker yet was born the son of a middle-class shop owner, its narrative purpose within the context and complex argument of 'An Elliptical Stylus' becomes much clearer. But first, let us return to the poem's narrative. The fourth and final stanza returns to deflated son and father, driving home from the shop 'slowly, as if we had a puncture', with 'my Dad trying not to blink, and that man's laugh / stuck in my head' (*SP* 11). This, too, we are told, is where 'the story sticks', and where the poem's argument comes to the fore. The loose rhyme scheme and forceful rising metre underline the poet-narrator's refusal of

> any attempt to cauterize this fable
> with something axiomatic on the nature
> of articulacy and inheritance,
> since he can well afford to make his *own*
> excuses, you your own interpretation.
> But if you still insist on resonance –
> I'd swing for him, and every other cunt
> happy to let my father know his station,
> which probably includes yourself. To be blunt. (*SP* 11)

Having carefully developed an emotive familial recollection (now crucially labelled a 'fable', as if to suggest its possible, though nonetheless purposeful, artifice) it seems odd that the poem should deny – or at least seem to want to deny – the reader a pithy, summarising conclusion. As one critic has questioned: 'What else is such a poem for, if not "something axiomatic on the nature / of articulacy and inheritance"?'[23] Paterson's own thoughts go some way towards illuminating the situation:

The poem ... was intended as a deliberate inversion of the current practice of inviting the audience to 'share' the experience; I'm terrified some well-heeled wee bugger will come up to me afterwards and tell me how much he enjoyed it. I think there are some grudges which need to be renewed annually; poetry is a good way of making palatable things that should remain indigestible, making certain kinds of crime easier for both the perpetrator and the victim to live with. There are a lot of sub-Tony Harrison types about who see their poetry as lending dignity to the working-class experience ... when what they're really dealing with is their own embarrassment with their social origins, and their awkwardness in using the language of their superiors. It's depressing to see the working-classes patronise *themselves* in this way.[24]

This correlates with a somewhat cautious reading of the poem's 'aesthetic poise' as 'a retrospective "swing" for the salesman'.[25] The final reversion to a stereotypically working-class response of aggression is viewed to be the result of a dissatisfaction with the poem's earlier appropriation of measured, stereotypically middle-class poetic technique. Apparently, this leaves the poem on the defensive and with a desire to 'out-articulate you, the reader, and then perhaps swing for you anyway'.[26] But the most illuminating reading of the poem must surely pay attention to the poem's central paradox. In both its refusal *and* acceptance to offer the reader a conclusive moral, it adopts a stance that is both in line with, and a volte-face of, that 'deliberate inversion ... of inviting the audience to "share" the experience'.

The poem's defining feature is the manner in which it continually remains one step ahead of the reader. It achieves this in a typically Patersonian estrangement of everyday detail, but also with its insistence on direct address to the reader, and its use of personae. To begin with, the reader is comfortably ensconced within the poem's commonplace mise en scène and class dynamic. But in convincingly adopting the persona of a stereotypically middle-class poet, the poem conjures its parenthetical parallel world, destabilising the emotive anecdote that precedes it. The poem then withholds the fable's expected précis, before the poet-speaker threatens to 'swing' for us, employing a direct address that insists on a more attentive, active, and clear-eyed engagement with the poem. The poem becomes a gauntlet, thrown down to any reader who thinks of poetry, as Paterson has put it in a lecture on the art form, as 'a kind of straight-faced recognition comedy', having 'no need either for originality or epiphany'.[27] In this way, the everyday yet unstable world of 'An Elliptical Stylus' refuses to reflect the comfortable perceptions and reductive preconceptions a reader may bring to it.

As readers, of course, we do continue to make instinctive stereotypical class-bound judgements of the characters the poem depicts. This is partly encouraged and directed by the poem itself: note its crafted and crafty use of language, but also its foregrounding of our anticipated judgements, and surface refusal to deliver the tale's expected neat summary. Yet, while the poem does not make plain its truths on 'the nature of articulacy and inheritance', they can be found within the poem, if the reader is willing to look for them. Aggressive it may be, but the 'resonance' provided in the poem's closing lines can be viewed as less a recourse to stereotypical working-class inarticulacy, and more an imperative to think interrogatively about what a poem depicts and suggests. The poet-speaker may appear willing to espouse a comfortable stereotype for the reader who refuses to see beyond simplifying class boundaries, but the implication is that such a reader misses the poem's purpose, if that is what they 'insist'. 'An Elliptical Stylus' therefore demands an understanding: neither the poem, nor its supposed moral or message, can be paraphrased, precisely because its transformative effect only functions when the reader is fully engaged in the demanding act of reading and thinking.

Alongside *Nil Nil*'s explorations of the constructed and mutable nature of the self, many of the book's poems reveal a recurrent fascination with the indistinct divide between reality and its copy. In 'The Ferryman's Arms', 'Morning Prayer', and 'An Elliptical Stylus' the concept of identity as unwavering, unified, and stable is put under the interrogative pressure of the poem's language to reveal it as an ungraspable, variable, and often externally inscribed construct. Similarly, a poem such as 'Next to Nothing' departs from a conventional understanding of reality and its copy – wherein the latter is a faithful representation of the former, akin to the classical concept of artistic *mimesis* – to reveal that the real and the imaginary are in fact much more intimately intertwined.

'Next to Nothing' is a vignette that depicts a deserted railway station. It opens with a disturbing image in this uncanny setting, suggesting that time has come to a standstill: 'The platform clock stuck on the golden section: / ten to three. A frozen sun' (*NN* 34). This mention of the golden section seems particularly significant. As a mysterious ratio that has fascinated philosophers, mathematicians, scientists, and artists since Euclid's geometrical treatise *Elements*, it gestures towards the often strange laws that appear to govern the universe and so, again, to Paterson's poetry's insistence on defamiliarising and making renewed sense of the world. This is literally echoed in the poem's description of 'the dead / acoustic of a small county', providing further quotidian detail, while also paradoxically reinforcing the sense that the place the poem depicts is a non-place, bolstered by the thumping adjectival 'dead' at the end of the line. As such, absence both indicates and becomes a new model of presence within the poem. A distant, unseen dog is reduced to its bark, which in turn is conjured as 'a short tear in the sky, above the wood', while the 'ghost of a lame porter / stabs a brush along the ground, then vanishes' (*NN* 34). Despite the poem's inversion of a traditional presence/absence hierarchy, however, at this point the sense of grounded reality remains. The poem's verisimilitude may be fraught with strangeness, but it is rooted within the realms of the typical and unremarkable. It is only when the scene's apparent adherence to the balancing ratio of the golden section is broken that the poem enacts its full transformation.

The poem's underlying argument appears to be in dialogue with disparities in accounts of this puzzling ratio. Whereas the German psychologist Adolf Zeising has suggested that the golden section represents a universal law 'in which is contained the ground-principle of all formative striving for beauty and completeness in the realms of both nature and art, and which permeates ... all structures, forms and proportions',[28] George Markowsky has argued that 'much of what is presented about the section in art, architecture, literature, and aesthetics is false or seriously misleading'.[29] In Paterson's 'Next to Nothing', the specific suggestion is that when the world is seen to depart from such a fundamentally – and therefore narrowly – human model of rationalising phenomena, a glimpse of the chaos lurking beneath our constricted perceptions is offered. Consequently, the apparent deterioration of all things towards nothingness, given the entropic laws that govern the matter of the universe, begins to occur.[30] 'The clock puts on a minute' and 'tips the balance', as the previously 'fixed stars' in the poem 'fall as dust' and (just as disturbingly, albeit less galactically) 'birdsong thaws in the air' (*NN* 34). The poem has segued from a vaguely strange verisimilitude to a jolting unreality in tellingly effortless manner. It is telling because this sense of unreality has stemmed from grounded reality itself: the quotidian setting of a railway station that, while quietly uncanny from the outset, is otherwise ordinary.

At this point, the poem's final line complicates things further, as across the station announcement system 'the recorded voice addresses its own echo'. This completes the deconstruction of a presence/absence hierarchy, and in turn the hierarchy of the real and its unreal copy. The recorded voice simultaneously gestures towards the absence of its origin while also asserting its presence and consequent independence from any origin, addressing itself in a kind of self-guaranteeing feedback loop. In rendering any simplistic concept of reality untenable, reality and unreality blur in 'Next to Nothing' to the extent that everything begins to feel unreal. This is the fullest sense of the poem's title. The deserted railway station is demonstrably 'next to nothing', but so too is everything else, since our modern perspectives on all landscapes are prone to the effects of hyperreal simulation. As the aphorist Antonio Porchia, mentioned in the prologue as a decisive influence on Paterson's poetry, reflects: 'Sometimes I think that everything I see does not exist. Because everything I see is what I saw. And everything that I saw does not exist.'[31] In a paradoxical yet clarifying sense that has ramifications throughout the rest of Paterson's oeuvre, 'Next to Nothing' uncovers how nothingness can come to engulf everything that the human mind perceives, and how everything is consequently revealed to be nothing in terms of how it is perceived. To quote Porchia again: 'When I believe that the stone is stone and the cloud cloud, I am in a state of unconsciousness.'[32]

'Next to Nothing's surface nihilism offers up the poem as a snapshot of paralysis. Indeed, *Nil Nil*'s overall atmosphere, along with the immediate sense and tenor of its poems, can appear unremittingly disturbing, bleak, despairing, haunted, and, at times, nightmarish. This is accentuated by the foreshortened and enigmatic nature of a number of its sonnets, near-sonnets, and vignettes, what Patrick Crotty keenly notes as the result of Paterson's 'desire to foster mystery in the attempt to supply a stylistic equivalent for the pervasive theme of estrangement'.[33] Whether coincidental or not, the phrase 'nil nil' visually contracts to 'nihil' and, in this sense, the book's title is grimly tautological: it could as well be *Nil*. And yet, *Nil Nil* also functions as a double negative, in which case the opposite is true: *Nil Nil* is everything. At the basic level of the deceptively simple phrasing of a book's title, Paterson's work offers a provocative paradox, evincing a complexity that undermines any simplistic critical engagement. If everything, or in other words, the entirety of the universe, comes from nothing (the gravitational singularity that existed prior to the Big Bang), and consequently everything is expanding yet at the same time decaying, in turn, everything will eventually become nothing again.[34] At first glance, these astrophysical connotations may seem far-fetched, but consider how the title's immediate suggestion of a football score (grounded, as ever, in the quotidian) conjures an everyday microcosm of this decay at work, or rather, at play. In spite of the frenetic activity on the pitch and in the stands during the game, the score is identical, and the field of play equally empty, at the end as it is at the beginning of a 0–0 draw. Like a nil–nil football game – both exciting and disappointing, eventful yet unresolved, everything and nothing – *Nil Nil* resists, at every turn, any reductive interpretation that would prevent its deadly serious play from exposing the inherent otherness of the ostensibly ordinary.

Nil Nil ends with its title poem, the sped-up tale of a fictitious football team's inglorious decline. 'From the top, then, the zenith, the silent footage: / McGrandle, majestic in ankle-length shorts', the poem renders in dismally hilarious detail 'the descent into pitch-sharing, / pay-cuts, pawned silver, the Highland Division, / the absolute sitters ballooned over open goals' (*SP* 18). Yet, at the same time, by deploying Paterson's characteristic blend of the everyday, the surreal, and the mystical, the poem represents a search for ontological significance. In the epigraph for 'Nil Nil', for instance, the fabricated presence of François Aussemain offers a lofty persona for Paterson's more avowedly philosophical thoughts, musing on 'those ignoble lines of succession that end in neither triumph nor disaster, but merely plunge on into deeper and deeper obscurity', while the poem's plot is eventually *'thinned down to a point so refined / not even the angels could dance on it'* (SP 19). In essence, this final poem is an echoing coda to much of that which has preceded it: namely, poems in which Paterson's perpetual face-off between routine encounters with the world, and the sense that the complex nature of reality lies beyond the perceptually restricted state of human consciousness, have begun to play out.

Consequently, with a swift *'Goodbye'*, Paterson's first collection leaves the reader behind, though not without having made a considerable impression. The poems' subtle cultivation of metaphysical paradox, drawn from the specific details of the everyday, frequently set into motion perceptual transformations that offer striking perspectives on the human condition and the reality we inhabit. This inventive use of quotidian detail is augmented, in poems such as 'An Elliptical Stylus', by the tentative use of poetic personae and direct address to the reader – stylistic features that, as we shall see, are exhibited in Paterson's later work with greater flexibility and prowess. In *Nil Nil*, they emerge as part of a burgeoning sense of poetry's function as a mode of knowledge. The collection ends with an instruction for the reader to *'get off'* the poem's slowing train of thought, with the poet declaring that he will *'continue alone, on foot, in the failing light'* (SP 19). The promise seems to be that Paterson's next book of poems will extend and expand the journey into considerably darker territory.

2

Which Man I Am:
God's Gift to Women (1997)

Paterson's early poems often concern themselves with the fluid and malleable nature of the self. While they interrogate notions of identity as stable and coherent, however, they do so almost entirely from the perspective of a broadly consistent persona. As Vicki Bertram has not unfairly summarised, the speaker in Paterson's early work tends to be 'an alienated and asocial bachelor: the solitary drinker, greeting the dawn by pissing from his window, recollecting shags from his past, troubled by his mortality, disgusted by procreation'.[1] But the anticipation and directing of the reader's expectations in a poem such as 'An Elliptical Stylus', and the self-reflexive, brisk dismissal of the speaker's audience at the close of 'Nil Nil', reveal how Paterson's first published poems also demonstrate an unusually keen understanding of poetry's inescapable artifice – the fullest sense of a poem as 'a made thing', from the Greek *poíēma*.

In spite of the dependable characterisation of the speaker in these poems, then, it would be misleading to view Paterson's work as concerned with mere recherché explorations of personal identity. Aspects of these early poems appear to suggest a deep-rooted fascination with the ways in which poetry not only serves to question reified notions of the self, but how the art form actively constructs and deconstructs believable identities – how even the most apparently autobiographical poem cannot help but deploy a persona that, while gesturing towards a flesh-and-bones speaker, remains, paradoxically, no more than a dramatised representation. As Peter Robinson has noted, in attempting to discuss the complex selves and situations that poems can often present, 'I don't believe that the speaker of a poem has to be a living, or once living, person ... yet for communication to take place representations have to be representations of *something*.'[2] In other words, the illusion of the presence of the poet within a poem is made possible by that poem's conjuring of the illusion of the present moment. Poems may utilise language in such ways as to gesture towards an immediacy that, in turn, gives rise to the seeming presence of a very real speaker.

Paterson recognises the manner in which interactions between poem and reader are governed by this strange set of circumstances. Not only has he spoken of the poem as an 'act of collusion',[3] but he has repeatedly expressed his belief that a poet should never 'confuse the voice of the poem with your own voice, because you're just limiting what you're capable of doing'.[4] The dynamic use of personae in Paterson's second collection, *God's Gift to Women*, evinces this, and is doubtless what has led some critics to variously label the volume as 'highly self-conscious',[5] 'incorrigibly post-modernist',[6] and marked by 'sleight-of-hand ... as an attempt by Paterson to distance himself from his subject'.[7] Yet while Robert Potts is right to describe *God's Gift to Women* as 'a book which plays obsessively with the vatic delivery of narrative or fiction', it would be ill-advised to dismiss Paterson's inventive use of personae as merely 'wasting itself in play and disguise'.[8] As close readings reveal, what William Scammell has termed Paterson's 'intention to take switchback rides on all the registers, and daring us to follow'[9] is most fully appreciated as a perceptually transformative attempt to unpick subject matter from a range of perspectives.

Though it has attracted sceptical criticism since it was first published during Modernism's heyday in the 1920s, it is difficult to exaggerate the enduring influence of T. S. Eliot's essay 'Tradition and the Individual Talent'. On the one hand, in arguing that a poet's significance lies in 'the appreciation of his relation to the dead poets and artists ... of the existing order ... of English literature',[10] Eliot's reductive notions of Tradition and the Canon (rather than plural traditions and canons) may appear to modern readers as hierarchical and hegemonic. But, on the other, his suggestion that the mature poet commits himself to a 'process of depersonalisation', and that 'the progress of an artist is a continual self-sacrifice, a continual extinction of personality',[11] is not so easily dismissed. Where a number of the experiments with personae in *God's Gift* are concerned, the essay's influence as theoretical underpinning to Paterson's increasingly sophisticated range of poetic voice is amply in evidence. Just as Eliot claims that 'poetry is not a turning loose of emotion, but an escape from emotion; it is not the expression of personality, but an escape from personality',[12] Paterson has stated in interview:

> It's a tremendously liberating day in a poet's life when you suddenly realise you can make it all up; the idea that poetry involves a fidelity to one's own experience and emotions is much more deeply engrained than you suspect – it operates almost as a moral imperative, so the first time you put words into someone's mouth, or kill off an aunt or uncle, it feels deliciously sinful.[13]

'11:00: Baldovan', part of a sporadic sequence in *God's Gift* structured around the haphazard schedule of a discontinued railway line, can be seen to align Paterson with Eliot's sense that the poet must 'surrender himself wholly to the work',[14] enacting a dismantling of the self. A tale of youthful dislocation, the poem employs the persona of the poet's childhood self, describing a trip with another boy, Ross Mudie, as the two go 'up the Hilltown / for the first time ever on our own' (*SP* 30). In a characteristic defamiliarisation of its quotidian setting, it evokes the queasiness of juvenile anxiety: the two boys await the arrival of the local bus at 'Base Camp' in 'horizontal sleet', raising 'the steel flag of the 20 terminus' as if they were about to embark on a dangerous mountaineering expedition. Even the speaker's pocket money has a sinister appearance – 'the cold blazonry of a half-crown', 'threepenny bits / like thick cogs', 'black pennies' – recalling the recurrent use of coin imagery in *Nil Nil*. As discussion of 'The Ferryman's Arms' in the previous chapter revealed, this symbolic paying of the ferryman's fee often signals Paterson's attempt to not only traverse the divide between life and death, but to expose these two conditions as less riven than the veil of human perception suggests. As Paterson has argued elsewhere: 'Man is probably unique amongst the mammals in that he has conscious foreknowledge of his own death. Knowing he will die means he acts, in part, as if he were already dead' (*O* 68).

In '11:00: Baldovan', this notion of the defining feature of human consciousness can be seen to find its fullest paradigm in the 'obscurely worried' persona of the young poet. In repeatedly asking his friend the same questions 'over matters of procedure, the protocol of travel', the highly sensitive speaker embodies an innocence that, through the course of the poem, paradoxically leads him to see both himself and his surroundings with a strangely renewed sense of flux. This occurs when the speaker's imagination takes a riotous turn, blurring reality with a vision of destruction, in which 'the bus will let us down in another country', a disorienting place 'with the wrong streets and streets that suddenly forget / their names at crossroads or in building-sites' (*SP* 30). As the poem progresses, this barren and confusing landscape further deteriorates in reaction to the narrator's escalating fears, an atmosphere conveyed by the gathering pace of the poem's metre, along with the sudden abandonment of conventional punctuation. The poem's unnerving segue from the habitual everyday to the darkly visionary suggests the ways in which fantastical imaginings can be as valid and intuitively true as the reified, language-dependent nature of consensual reality.

Yet '11:00: Baldovan' does not serve to primarily undermine such simplified notions of the real. Rather, the tangible scenes the poem constructs and unpicks, moving from innocence to experience – from the speaker's whimsical wish 'to buy comics, / sweeties, and magic tricks', to a fragmented world in which the family home has been destroyed and his loved ones are deceased – both facilitate and mirror the creation and disintegration of the persona at its core. The aforementioned agency of the poem's landscape, engendering its own destruction, can be seen as a metaphor for the quite deliberate collapse of the young speaker's fragile sense of self. In the believable yet disquieting world the poem conjures, this process emerges from the narrator's anxious dread. But we also get the impression that the poet (who inevitably also occupies the poem's dramatised voice) is quite consciously playing with this persona. As Eliot argues: 'There is a great deal, in the writing of poetry, which must be conscious and deliberate.'[15]

In '11:00: Baldovan', the assertion that 'I'm weighing up my spending power' can be seen as much a reference to the speaker's pocketful of coins as to the poet's sense of authorial command. It is no coincidence that the knowing poet laments his childhood persona's constant fretting ('I cannot know the little good it will do me'), immediately before the world that defines that character's sense of self speedily disintegrates. The poem may see Paterson afford that reimagined early self – and by extension, the reader – the somewhat dubious benefit of hard-won insight. But it is authorial experimentation with that persona that appears to supply the poem's governing force, conjuring a credible identity only to unravel it. In deploying and almost destroying a seemingly autobiographical approxi-mation of his childhood self, Paterson makes the poem a site for exploring the poet's heightened sense of the 'twin citizenship' of human life and death (*O* 69). According to Paterson, mankind has become 'so accustomed to living in death's shadow … he barely notices that, while contingency and fate might shape his life, it is death that drives its plot' (*O* 68). It is the poet, he claims, who can 'live in the heart of the paradox itself, forming a stereoscopic view of the world with one eye in the land of the living and one eye in the land of the dead'. In '11:00: Baldovan', Paterson begins to test the possibilities and limits of poetic personae, a project in line with Eliot's concept of poetry, as Maud Ellman succinctly describes it, as 'the workshop of the self, where personal identity is both constructed and dismantled'.[16]

While '11:00: Baldovan' sees Paterson creatively deploying and undoing a single poetic self, another poem in *God's Gift*, 'Candlebird', pushes the book's experimentation with personae further, conjuring several dramatised and competing identities at once. A sonnet that loosely reworks a verse by the medieval Arabic poet Abbas Ibn Al-Ahnaf, the poem draws on the latter's melancholic fascination with the changeable iterability of the love lyric, in particular the idea that where the poet may fail to impress the beloved with his crafted words, another could succeed through borrowing and repeating them. 'If, tonight, she scorns me for my song, / You may be sure of this', laments Paterson's lovelorn poet-speaker: 'within the year / Another man will say this verse to her / And she will yield to him for its sad sweetness' (*SP* 52). Unlike Ibn Al-Ahnaf's more straightfor-wardly direct address from poet-speaker to the second-person 'you' of the beloved,[17] however, 'Candlebird' interlaces a complex web of cajoling voices. This confounds any attempt to identify the poem, and the mise en abyme of its poems-within-poems, with an individual and coherent self:

> *"'Then I am like the candlebird'"*, he'll continue,
> After explaining what a candlebird is,
> *"'Whose lifeless eyes see nothing and see all,*
> *Lighting their small room with my burning tongue;*
>
> *His shadow rears above hers on the wall*
> *As hour by hour, I pass into the air."*
> Take my hand. Now tell me: flesh or tallow?
> Which I am tonight, I leave to you.'
>
> So take my hand and tell me, flesh or tallow.
> Which man I am tonight I leave to you. (*SP* 52)

In Ibn Al-Ahnaf's original, the poet-speaker compares himself to a candle, suggesting that his words are destined to illuminate the sexual conquests of other men, rather than his own. Paterson's 'Candlebird' preserves this implication, but the simile is made more specific, invoking a particular type of seabird whose flesh is so saturated in oil it may be threaded with a wick and burnt. Coupled with the ironic manner in which this is presented – the beloved's suitor speaks the lines as if they were his, while the quotation marks and italicisation make clear that they are the work of the poet-speaker – this suggests an image of the poem as a flighty creature, possessing a life of its own that will always escape the intentions and desires of its author. Indeed, even the poet-speaker's 'original' poem is a version adapted from another. But, at the same time, the deceased and threaded candlebird also implies the damaging effects of any attempt to tether the poem to a limited conception of its speaker, particularly one that is an autobiographical approximation of its author. Having lamented his failure to court his love interest by singing the work himself, the poet-speaker's quoting of his lines as they are successfully spoken by another suggests how an audience's interpretation of any poem is subject to their notion of the persona that appears to deliver it.

But while the emotional texture of 'Candlebird' seems forlorn and resigned – the poet-speaker accepts the manner in which he, and those who quote his lines, are at the mercy of the lover's (or reader's) subjective apprehension – the sonnet's final couplet also serves to recast the poem as a statement of intent. Stripped of the second and third stanza's metatextual quotation marks and italicisation, these final lines might appear to return the poem to the bereft voice of the poet-speaker in the first quatrain. But their near-identical repetition of the prior lines, as spoken by the beloved's suitor, deviates in one crucial detail. Where the 'other man' seductively implores that it is up to his lover whether she finds him, and his borrowed verses, to be 'flesh or tallow' (which is to say authentic and worthy of approbation, or else inauthentic and 'lifeless'), the poet-speaker extends this demand to conflate his own presence with that of the successful suitor, reaching out instead to the reader. '"Which I am tonight, I leave to you"' becomes 'Which *man* I am tonight I leave to you': shorn of its quotation marks, this final line directly addresses and so involves the reader in the poem-as-dialogue, while also reinforcing Paterson's concept of a poem's creative agency and the 'act of collusion' between poem and reader. As he has argued in his *ars poetica*: 'the poem ... demands the complicity of the reader in its own creation'.[18] We as readers are left to decide, based on its lyric economies, whether or not the poem evokes a convincing speaker whose conjured presence ensures its emotional and intellectual significance.

The implication here is that it is not any connection with an actual, or even once, living person that ensures a poem's authenticity and success. Rather, it is the poem's creation of the apparent presence of a convincing human being, its manipulation of language to impart the illusion of the present moment. 'You may be sure of this'; 'Take my hand'; 'Now tell me'; 'Which I am tonight I leave to you': the poem constantly issues imperatives and directly addresses the reader, encouraging us to recognise the active role we play in the construction of the poem, as much as it may direct and subtly dictate the ways in which we do so. Like John Keats's 'This Living Hand', where the once 'warm and capable / Of earnest grasping' is reanimated by our reading into the poem's illusion of the present, Paterson's poem is, on one level, an attempt to bridge the gap between the urgency of the moment of poetic composition and the words as we find them on the page, in the head or on the tongue of a reader – years, decades, perhaps even centuries later. 'And thou be conscience-calmed', writes Keats, 'see here it is – / I hold it towards you'.[19]

While as readers we apprehend the conjured presence of the dual persona in 'Candlebird' just as we see Keats's gesturing hand, however, there is a difference. Keats's poem attempts to discover aspects of the system of language – how it is that poems are made with, and succeed through, words rather than ideas. But this occurs against the bedrock of a reassuringly coherent poetic persona; there is no suggestion in 'This Living Hand', for example, that the self that extends its hand through the poem is compromised beyond its direct, physical counterpart inevitably ending up 'cold / And in the icy silence of the tomb'. The impression is that the hand in the poem is the straightforwardly mimetic equivalent to Keats's actual hand buried in a cemetery in Rome, revivified by the poem's conjuring trick. Poem and poet form a continuum. This is not the case in 'Candlebird'. Here we see Paterson go further than Eliot's poetics of impersonality and the willed workshopping of the self. It is a poem that uncovers the manner in which the creative process inevitably undoes the self, since that self is made from nothing more than the fluid medium of language. The poem evinces Eliot's 'process of depersonalisation', but it again shares striking affinities with the work of the Symbolist poet Stéphane Mallarmé. 'The work of the pure poetry implies the elocutionary disappearance of the poet, who yields the initiative to words',[20] Mallarmé claimed; 'it is in front of the paper that the artist creates himself'.[21] As Barthes argues in 'The Death of the Author':

> Mallarmé was doubtless the first to see and to foresee in its full extent the necessity to substitute language itself for the person who until then had been supposed to be its owner. For him, for us too, it is language which speaks, not the author; to write is, through a prerequisite impersonality ... to reach that point where only language acts, 'performs', and not 'me'.[22]

Though it frames and partly disguises it through its emotively persuasive tale of seduction, this is the real subject of 'Candlebird'. 'I believe in poems, not poets, so sod the individual voice' Paterson has written in an *ars poetica* essay accompanied by this very poem, and while speaking in playfully combative fashion, it is also clearly a stalwart belief of his, reiterated elsewhere in his critical writings. 'A poet should be in service to the poem', he states, 'and while that's the case, nothing exists except the poem; the poem annihilates the poet'.[23] It is telling that 'Candlebird' is the penultimate poem in God's Gift to Women, followed only by 'Siesta', the first of Paterson's many translated versions after the Spanish poet Antonio Machado, collected in his third volume The Eyes. As will be further discussed in this chapter and the next, it is through having variously pushed the limits of poetic personae that Paterson eventually grants himself license to inhabit and reimagine Machado's 'singerless song' (TE 59), attempting to create poems both autonomous and anonymous where, as Michael Wood has noted, 'the poet is not a forlorn artist or a suffering everyman, and not even, essentially, a projection of the historical person of the poet, but the agent of a lyrical intelligence to which we could all aspire'.[24]

As 'Candlebird' suggests, in God's Gift to Women Paterson's serious play with personae is amply in evidence. It is a technique that allows Paterson to explore the way in which language, rather than the author, speaks within a poem, but also in order to scrutinise those most crucial aspects of identity: gender and sexuality. 'Paterson's is a technically insightful and violent imagination', Robert Crawford has noted of God's Gift to Women: 'Callousness and damage get mixed up with sex and gender in many poems.'[25] God's Gift to Women can be seen as an attempt to interrogate issues of gender and sexuality by means of ironically perpetuating traditional modes of representation – the dominant, aggressive, and sometimes cruel nature of the masculine, as pitched against the submissiveness and emotional fragility of the feminine – rather than overtly fragmenting and destabilising such conventions. But in doing so, the poems can run the risk of merely replicating and endorsing, rather than parodying and so subverting these representations. As Vicki Bertram notes: 'The predilection for bathos and the jokey games symptomatic of postmodernist antics are presumably meant to make the poems amusing, but the humour – because it depends on irony alone – is coercive.'[26] However, Bertram's subscription to the 'foundationalism' of feminist identity politics – fixing and constraining the reified genders of the very identities she presumably hopes to liberate – leads her to read many of the poems in God's Gift to Women in a rather straightforwardly blinkered fashion, ignoring their dramatised speakers and scenarios in favour of viewing such poems as evidence of the barely veiled misogynistic intent of the poet 'behind' them. 'In this volume', she declaims, 'lies and savage irony provide perfect cover for a fully postmodern display of masculinity'.[27] In other words, *God's Gift to Women* apparently finds a macho poet indulging in chauvinism and chest-thumping, with the parody and irony of the poems a smokescreen.

This critical position does many of the poems a disservice, ignoring the way in which Paterson's parodic use of dramatis personae can allow for a transformative unpicking of conventional depictions of gender and sexuality. If a poem such as *'from* 1001 Nights: The Early Years', reimagining an early scene from the framing tale of *The Arabian Nights* (*SP* 27), ultimately fails to transform conventional notions of gender and sexuality by replicating rather than undermining and reinventing them, 'Imperial', a thematically similar yet stylistically distinct poem in *God's Gift to Women*, cannot be so easily dismissed. An account of a couple's first sexual encounter and accompanying emotional repercussions, this poem sets up a familiar conceptual metaphor – love is war – in the stylistic context of a traditional yet disrupted poetic form: an alternating rhyme scheme in metered quatrains that comes to dispense with conventional punctuation. Unlike *'from* 1001 Nights: The Early Years', this suggests from the outset that the poem's constructed persona will serve to challenge the very patriarchal male viewpoint and male-dominated lyric tradition it puts into motion. In subtly subversive fashion, the poem opens with the voice of the beloved – *'Is it normal to get this wet? Baby, I'm frightened'* – who is then quickly and ironically silenced, as per the conventions of the Renaissance love lyric: 'I covered her mouth with my own' (*SP* 48). The couple then have sex, but only 'after months of jaw jaw, determined that neither / win ground, or be handed the edge'. 'We gave ourselves up', laments the speaker, 'one to the other / like prisoners over a bridge':

> and no trade was ever so fair or so tender;
> so where was the flaw in the plan,
> the night we lay down on the flag of surrender
> and woke on the flag of Japan (*SP* 48)

Just as the masculine persona in 'Imperial' is seemingly authoritative, the muted feminine character appears submissive and hesitant. But both come to depart from the gender identities assigned them in the poem's first stanza. The poem's calculated and clinical poise in dealing with matters of intimacy might initially recall the sceptical intelligence associated with the amorous poetry of the seventeenth-century Metaphysical poet John Donne. 'They are ours as fruits are ours' wrote Donne in 'Community', in a characteristic conceit that intellectualises the manner in which men might sexually 'devour' women: 'And when he hath the kernel eat, / Who doth not fling away the shell?'[28] But where Donne's poem exhibits the male bigotry of his age in its philosophical play, 'Imperial' clearly interrogates its own stance. Paterson's speaker is not cocksure in the manner of Donne's, and not boastful; tinged with irony, the tone is broadly one of weary resignation. Moreover, the silencing of the lover by the male speaker before 'she lay in my arms' is short-lived, giving way to the 'storm-window' above their bed, 'stood at our heads like a stone'. This decisively turbulent and morbid image not only indicates that war will play vehicle to love's tenor in the poem's metaphorical conceit, but that both parties will pay the price of their strategised consummation, failing to achieve more than a shallow resolution, much as once warring nations count their fallen dead in the cemeteries. Rather than a merely conventional scenario of passive female yielding to domineering male, 'Imperial' suggests that both are engaged in tactical 'jaw jaw', 'determined that neither / win ground'.

In this manner, the poem's argument displays a clear affinity with the gender theorising of Judith Butler, particularly her persuasive idea that genders are fundamentally performative. According to Butler, 'acts, gestures, and desire produce the effect of an internal core or substance', giving rise to the illusion of genders as static entities, rather than the surfaces without fixity or substance that they truly are.[29] 'The radical dependency of the masculine subject on the female "Other" suddenly exposes his autonomy as illusory': Butler has thus argued for the destabilising effect of female agency on male authority,[30] an argument with which Paterson's 'Imperial' not only appears to concur, but one that it imaginatively enacts. In the poem, it is not simply masculine dominance but the persistent constructs of both masculine and feminine stereotypes that sullies sex, transforming what should be a loving act of intimacy into a cautious tussle towards a truce, akin to prisoners traded 'over a bridge' in the name of imperial control. As such, 'no trade was ever so fair or so tender' is perhaps the most fiercely ironic line in the entire poem (*SP* 48). There is little fair, and certainly nothing tender, about a physical act that embodies no emotional intimacy. Equally, the knowing lack of a question mark in the following line – 'so where was the flaw in the plan' – lends the statement a rhetorical hollowness. By now, both poet and reader know exactly where the flaw is: it lies in the very fact that there was a plan, borne of a cautious hostility between two lovers who are unable to break free from damaging gender stereotypes.

The poem may on certain levels allow for the 'parodic displacement' that Butler calls for, creating 'a context ... in which subversive confusions can be fostered ... to compel a reconsideration of the place and stability of the masculine and the feminine'[31]. But its final, beautifully worded, yet ultimately grotesque image of two lovers laying down on 'the flag of surrender' only to wake on the virginally bloodied 'flag of Japan' seems to suggest, if anything, a renewal of imperial hostilities between parties. In 'Imperial', and in *God's Gift* more generally, Paterson is clearly engaged in exposing the dangers of a damaging and inflexible masculinity. But in spite of intelligently discussing the pathology of gender stereotypes through use of poetic personae, the poems seem to find little hope for future change – even when his writing is as its most sensitive, attuned, and philosophically discursive.

In poems that defamiliarise and question the everyday with subversive use of parody and irony, *God's Gift to Women* finds Paterson blending playful use of conventional forms with a variety of poetic personae. 'Imperial' does so in its interrogation of an atavistic masculinity, one that continues to pervade contemporary society and exert its effects on both personal and public footings. Yet, as the volume's title poem suggests, extending the search for transcendence and ontological significance first seen in *Nil Nil*'s title poem (not to mention 'the immaculate finish' of 'The Ferryman's Arms'), the word 'God' in *God's Gift to Women* is as important as the word 'Women'. Whether it materialises in the form of idealised father figure and Holy Father, or more often as an untenable yet yearned-for symbol of spiritual possibility and immaterial understanding, the lure of religion in the broadest sense is one that frequently ghosts the collection.

As Sean O'Brien has noted, with more than a little understatement: 'Like it or not, there is a residual religious element in Paterson's work.'[32] While Paterson's relationship with religion and the spiritual may be undeniable, however, it is far from straightforward. On the one hand, he clearly views the practice of writing poetry as a transcendental event – 'I'm absolutely scunnered with writers who refuse to acknowledge the spiritual dimension in their work', he once proclaimed.[33] But, on the other, his opinions of organised religion are negative and even damning, fed in part by formative experiences. Paterson's grandfather was a preacher in the United Reformed Church of Scotland, and in his youth, Paterson himself fell for the appeal of 'charismatic Christianity', memories that surely inform an early poem from *Nil Nil*, 'Amnesia', which takes as its initial point of departure the young speaker as 'a very sick boy', 'arms / outstretched in catatonic supplication' as he feigns speaking in tongues for the approval of church elders (*SP* 12). 'It was a horrific experience', Paterson later recounted of the time: 'And there were some responsible adults around who should not have been filling impressionable minds with that sort of bullshit.'[34] The tension – and the distinction – here is one between a distrust of the potentially misleading, dogmatic dangers of organised religion, and the appeal of the genuine, perception-altering potential of spiritual receptivity.

'Prologue' is the opening poem in *God's Gift to Women*. As such, its title suggests that it can be read as a preface, setting the tone for the rest of the book – though taking things at face value in *God's Gift to Women* is, as seen, always a potentially perilous approach. What can be said for certain is that 'Prologue' draws a distinction between the transformative power of a spiritually attuned poetry and the grandiose illusions of the finger-wagging church. This seriously witty poem opens with its speaker invoking himself – and by implied extension, a great many poems' speakers – as a self-important priest, intoning that 'a poem is a little church, remember, / you its congregation, I, its cantor' (*GG* 1). The poem exemplifies Paterson's ability to combine a quotidian setting with heightened direct address, transporting the reader from ordinariness to otherness. But while this is true, and contributes to 'Prologue's success in both undermining and enacting two different modes of 'spiritual transport' – namely, that of prescribed religious dogma, and the transcendental release of genuine poetry – ironic humour and fluid use of persona are also key. This is evident in the poem's accomplished facility to both mock and exalt poetry and religion in equal measure, complicating our conventional understandings of both.

The priest-persona begins by chastising his audience, which is to say us readers, with a litany of restrictions – 'no flash, no necking in the pew, / or snorting just to let your neighbour know // you get the clever stuff, or eyeing the watch' – before requesting that we 'be upstanding'. 'Now', invites our preacher with a wink, 'let us raise the fucking *tone*' (*GG* 1). If this is a wry attack on the self-important dullness of the contemporary poetry reading, where a captive audience wriggle in their seats, as bored as a church congregation before a lecturing pastor, it is also a more literal call for that audience, and the reader, to sit up and pay attention, recognising that a poem is an act of communication that always requires a degree of seriousness and intellectual expenditure. As in his dealings with masculinity discussed in 'Imperial', Paterson again seems to be in dialogue with John Donne, particularly the Donne of *Anniversaries* and *Verse Letters*, who negotiates spiritual dilemmas with a similar mixture of scepticism and intellectual rigour, but also impassioned resolve: 'Our business is, to rectify / Nature, to what she was', he states in a belles-lettres 'To Sir Edward Herbert, at Juliers'.[35] The fault may often be with the poet and/or poem, the method of delivery, but equally it can lie with the audience, 'Prologue' suggests, and a lack of capacity or willingness to engage and question.

'Spiritual transport', then, as the poem puts it, is not a passively consumable experience. Just as discussion of 'An Elliptical Stylus' revealed Paterson demonstrating the sense in which poetry's imaginatively transformative effects only function through the act of attentive reading, 'Prologue' implies that access to poetry's spiritual capacity requires that very same focus and effort. Yet, we are told, the poem is destined to fail if it does not merit real attention: language in its 'least prestigious form', which is to say the 'less elevated' realm of the hymns and prayers of organised religion, is something for which Paterson has elsewhere expressed his distain. 'Prayer really is the lowest form of literature', he has claimed, 'desire and flattery are nowhere sung so nakedly' (*TBS* 118). But while the 'little church' of lyric poetry may be 'neither high nor broad', it can, if poem and reader are both up to the task, offer a less deceived and more questing and questioning spirituality to the dogma practised by the High or Broad Church (*GG* 2). It is this sentiment that surely informs the world-wearied, bluntly nihilistic close of 'Prologue', an 'Oh God' that sends up more zealous uses of that phrase, leading not into conventional prayer, but a falling into silence, bereft of a final full-stop. In this meditative quiet, the poem suggests – of the white space of the blank page, and the careful marks the poet makes upon it – true revelation and understanding might occur.

While Paterson may articulate this belief in 'Prologue', however, arguing for a meaningful, broadly spiritual poetry that is not apparent in the untenable rigidity of conventional notions of God and the unconvincing scriptures of organised religion, *God's Gift to Women* nonetheless finds poems that struggle to put this notion into practice. The title of 'On Going to Meet a Zen Master in the Kyushu Mountains and Not Finding Him', for example, may seem to suggest Buddhism as a more palatable religious alternative (*SP* 49). But in doing so, Paterson is only content to offer up a blank page as poem itself, playing with notions of presence and absence that do more to recall the *via negativa* or 'negative way' of ancient theology, an attempt to understand the divine by way of negation. Where Paterson's approach deviates from the *via negativa*, however, is in his pursuit of a genuine spiritualism that is without a godhead. The poem is 'missing' because, for Paterson, God – in a Nietzschean sense – has gone missing; it is also 'missing' much in the way that the Buddha, in a sutta from the scriptures, is said to have refused to answer questions about metaphysical propositions such as the existence of the soul and life after death: the Buddha suggests instead that understanding comes through questioning not what is, but what is not. For Paterson, insistence on a sceptical yet openly agnostic frame of mind requires that the spiritual be approached obliquely, and negative transcendence clearly offers one solution. As Crawford notes: 'Paterson has never forgiven his God for walking out, and the sense of emptiness at the heart of many of these minutely imagined and powerful poems adds to the nihilism which is twinned with verbal electricity.'[36] The collection finds Paterson still yearning after the spiritual, struggling towards an openly intuitive engagement with the world through language that can also allow for the guarding scepticism of a rigorously existential outlook.

3

Not Your Name, Not Mine:
The Eyes (1999)

If the poetry of *God's Gift to Women* documents the struggle
between Paterson's ludic tendencies and his increasingly
metaphysical and meditative sensibility, then *The Eyes*, his
third collection comprising loosely translated 'versions' after
the Spanish of Antonio Machado, can be seen as a neat
bypassing of this issue. As Peter Forbes has argued: 'The
conflict between Paterson's MacNeicean lyric streak and the
postmodernist demands of the age is not yet resolved', though
the poems in *The Eyes* 'neatly side-step the problem by using
someone else's poems that are unashamedly lyrical'.[1] But
there is an originality and force to Paterson's adaptations
of Machado that makes them much more than mere artistic
portraiture. 'Paterson's previous work might have prepared
us for the spiritual and lyrical kinship he so obviously shares
with Machado', as John Burnside argues, 'yet his achievement,
in *The Eyes*, is one that should not be taken for granted: these
are both versions and highly original poems, in a very real
sense, highly inventive solutions ... to a difficult and beautiful
problem'.[2]

The difficult and beautiful problem that Burnside alludes to
is one of artistic sensibility. As he rightly points out:

> Machado is not an obvious poet to offer an Anglo-Saxon audience:
> he demands that we set aside the notion that what matters – all
> that matters – is the social (the public and the personal, as it were)
> and insinuates the possibility that there really is an inner, asocial,
> individual soul, in the philosophical or religious sense, engaged in
> a spiritual journey.[3]

Machado is a poet of philosophical seriousness, who nevertheless makes a gentle mockery of the solipsistic Romantic notion of the sovereignty of the individual. It is not difficult to sense why Paterson, a poet committed to serious play with poetic voice and personae, should feel sympathy for a poet whose work exhibits lyrical coherence within a credo committed to anonymity, the artistic erasure of the self, and the poetic truths of paradox. As Alan Trueblood notes in introduction to his own translations of the Spanish poet: 'Machado's fidelity to his post-Romantic aesthetic, his penchant for philosophical speculation, and his growing commitment to a social role for art had made him an increasingly isolated figure.'[4] The same might be said to a certain extent of Paterson and his poetry, and in Machado he clearly admires what he sees as 'his bravery' – which for Paterson amounts to his plainness of expression, his complex thinking, and his emotional candour.[5] That, and the sense that 'there are several Antonio Machados, but I've only tried to write the poem Machado is for me, one about God and love and memory; to that extent *The Eyes* is really one poem' (*TE* 55). 'This poet of absences and distances', as Jamie McKendrick has labelled Machado,[6] informs Paterson's increasingly sophisticated attempts at self-abnegation, but also the further development of poems as a mode of knowledge, in which an openly intuitive, spiritual engagement with the world is balanced with the guarding rigour of a warily existential outlook.

In the previous chapter, we discussed how Paterson's serious play with poetic personae moves beyond T. S. Eliot's theory of impersonality as willed workshopping of the self, towards an aesthetic that finds poetry to be a process that inevitably undoes the self. Rather than attempting self-abnegation, in which the active avoidance of a coherent and reified poetic identity (typically bearing some perceived resemblance to its author) is likely to find said identity returning at a gallop, *God's Gift to Women*, and the poem 'Candlebird' in particular, illustrates Paterson's interest in what Mallarmé first described as 'the work of the pure poetry', one that entails 'the elocutionary disappearance of the poet, who yields the initiative to words'.[7] In Paterson's increasingly sophisticated understanding of this poetic technique, Antonio Machado makes for an apposite lyric ally. As Alan Trueblood has noted of the Spanish poet's work:

'He acknowledges an otherness within as well as without. The self becomes many-sided, extensible, resisting delimitation.'[8] Indeed, in his 'Afterword' to *The Eyes*, Paterson makes a similar point in favour of Machado's 'selfless' verse, before criticising those who would label such poetry 'postmodern':

> I can think of no writer so obsessed with the suppression of his own ego, and he would have been disappointed in any reader who sought to 'explain' a poem in terms of a geographic or psychological provenance ... The occasional intrusion of the discussion of the processes of art itself, no doubt some will call 'postmodern'. This self-reflexion, i.e. writing becoming aware of itself as writing, is a perennial and inevitable consequence of the serious play of the human imagination; 'postmodernism' is a literary tendency distinguished only by a self-conscious focus on this operation to the exclusion of others. This is to misread and diminish Machado; he writes of writing only to deny his part in it, a double paradox – as if Escher's hands held erasers, not pens. (*TE* 55–9)

This dismissal of the contemporary notion of the 'postmodern' – as needless critical foregrounding of the ubiquitous and age-old inevitability of linguistic play – is an interesting one. It doubtless speaks of Paterson's attempt to reconcile the tension between his own philosophically minded lyric tendencies with the ludic play he is also given to. The appeal of Machado's aesthetic is in large part to do with what Paterson views as the inherent purposefulness of Machado's self-reflexion, distinguishing him from those writers engaged in mere recherché postmodern games. The image of M. C. Escher's *Drawing Hands* lithograph – an artwork in which two hands are involved in the paradoxical act of drawing each other into existence – is invoked, but with a twist: Paterson sees Machado as engaged in the necessary process of self-erasure and, by extension, in poetic composition as an act that always finds that language, rather than any person or author, is doing the talking. And, since language is the ultimate communal medium, this in turn allows for a poetry that can legitimately assume a collective voice of shared thought and feeling – something that, as we have already touched on in previous chapters, Paterson is keen to reclaim in a modern poetic climate where careful subjectivity is all. Machado, he suggests, 'offers us the chance to make a quiet return to a poetry of moral instruction; a function contemporary poetry seems to have forgotten it ever performed but whose absence may well account for poetry's present irrelevance to the lives of many readers' (*TE* 59–60). As Trueblood argues of Machado's early work:

> The prominence ... of compositions in which the poet's individual voice seeks attunement to the collective voice of popular poetry ... is symptomatic of a continuing search for forms of expression facilitating communion with others and, more broadly, of a search for some meeting ground with the otherness of the world.[9]

The opening poem of *The Eyes*, 'Advice', is one of several miniature manifestos in the volume, whereby Paterson's *ars poetica* is gradually readjusted in the light of Machado's communally voiced, deeply reflective poetry. 'My advice?' the poem begins, as if the reader had asked for it, but with a nudge and a wink that recognises the peculiar conversational dynamic that exists between any poem and its audience. 'To watch, and wait for the tide to turn', the poem continues, 'wait as the beached boat waits' (*SP* 57). If the poem's anonymous voice is to be believed, it is only 'the patient' who succeed, getting ahead by their very dismissal of the urge to get ahead, knowing that a boat's departure will come as and when it comes. This proffered advice, of course, is as much general life advice as it is very specific advice to the artist – especially to the aspirant poet, eager for the false promise of lyric glory. But what of the speaker? 'As I put it so well myself', he self-mockingly boasts: '"The patient triumph / since life is long, and art merely a toy."' Quoting lines in order to conflate personae, confronting the fact that the apparent speaker of any poem is as easily undone as it is conjured: this is a trick that Paterson has already enacted in 'Candlebird'. Here, in the first poem of *The Eyes*, he is similarly quick to confuse and ultimately dismiss any assumed authorial identity the reader might reductively inscribe. It doesn't matter whether you think 'Paterson' or 'Machado' is doing the talking, the poem suggests: the importance lies in the poem's argument, the ideas it proposes and provokes, rather than in an authorial locus.

At the same time, these quoted lines at the end of the poem's first stanza harbour a fidelity to the original Spanish from which its final stanza, waiting in its own 'little boat', comes to depart.

'The only defensible fidelity is to the entirely subjective quality of "spirit" or "vision", rather than to literal meaning', Paterson argues in his 'Afterword' (*TE* 58) – whether or not you agree with such scepticism about the possibility of any real equivalences in the art of translation, it is this attitude that well equips him to craft original poems from his own readings of Machado. Unlike its inspirational source, Paterson's 'Advice' is cleaved into two five-line stanzas, and its second stanza is much more playfully didactic than the original:

> Well – okay – supposing life is short,
> and the sea never touches your little boat –
> just wait, and watch, and wait, for art is long;
> whatever. To be quite honest with you,
> none of this is terribly important. (*SP* 57)

Whereas Machado's original registers a tone of resilient hopefulness in the face of uncertainty and adversity[10] (in a more direct translation, Trueblood finds the poem stating that the reader should 'still wait and don't depart, go right on hoping'[11]), Paterson's poem finds its speaker offering this advice half-heartedly, with a dismissive 'whatever'. Moreover, the polite and slightly fussy diction of the poem's final clause does little to disguise its impatience with any reader, or ambitious poet, who is keen to get ahead. 'None of this is terribly important' might sound like a strange rejection of art and life – the poem's ostensible twin subjects – but, framed within a poem that adopts an anonymous and initially confident voice that comes to deliberately undermine its own vatic pronouncements, this statement in fact reveals that, up to a point, the only advice finally worth listening to is likely that of your own gut instinct. Patience is undeniably a virtue, but no one can tell you how long to wait, or when it is time to act, to make something happen. 'Set out from any point. They are all alike. They all lead to a point of departure',[12] states the aphorist Antonio Porchia, whose collection *Voices* furnishes Paterson with numerous epigraphs dotted throughout his work, and whose influence on Paterson may be accounted for by what W. S. Merwin has described as Porchia's 'witness to the private ordeal and awe of individual existence, the reality that is glimpsed through time and circumstance'.[13] This statement is of a kin with Paterson's refashioning of Machado here. 'Advice' seems to be about the Paterson of *God's Gift to Women*, of linguistic excess and 'postmodern' play, finding his 'little boat' suddenly stranded ashore, and wondering what comes next. As well as a poem with a genuine message about patience in the face of art's demands and life's desires, it also reads as a playfully didactic testing of Machadian waters, which Paterson's further engagements with the Spanish poet's poetics will negotiate more confidently.

If 'Advice' finds Paterson gently launching a 'little boat' into unfamiliar waters, then an emphatically titled sonnet, 'Poetry', represents a new manifesto in earnest. In this vignette, Paterson attempts to articulate the precise appeal of Machado's aesthetic, crafting a versioned refashioning of a late, key poem from the Spanish poet's oeuvre. As such, 'Poetry' picks up where Machado's poem steps off, beginning by invoking a metaphorical comparison between the 'steady' formation of the poem, and that of the 'mindless diamond' (*SP* 71). Just as the latter keeps its 'spark of the planet's early fires', we are told, trapped in its 'net of ice', 'it's not love's later heat that poetry holds, / but the atom of the love that drew it forth / from the silence'.

At first glance, this might suggest a Romantic poetic credo, inviting comparison with Wordsworth's Preface to the *Lyrical Ballads*, in which he famously argues that while poetry may be 'the spontaneous overflow of powerful feelings, it takes its origin from emotion recollected in tranquillity'.[14] But what differentiates Machado – and by extension, Paterson in his own take on Machado's poetics – from Romantic solipsism, is a commitment to a poetic voice of serene anonymity; or, at the very least, the aim for such a voice. Whereas Romanticism might be practically defined by the free expression and centrality of the feelings of the individual, for Machado and for Paterson it is a desire for the communal voice of language, not the artist, to do the talking that comes to govern the poetic project – and along with it, the hope of authentically capturing shared thoughts and feelings. In poetry, each feeling, Machado once stated, 'needs for its production the distress of other frightened hearts amid a nature not understood … In short, my feeling is not exclusively mine, but ours.'[15] 'So if the bright coal of his love / begins to smoulder', continues 'Poetry', 'the poet hears his voice suddenly forced … boastful / with his own huge feeling' (*SP* 71).

For Paterson, what is to be admired in Machado's work is this distaste for the excessive and decadent, for the kind of adorned writing that seeks only to sweeten the honey of true emotion. As Trueblood argues:

Machado is rarely truly self-deprecatory, and it is in self-affirmation, not self-pity, that he recognises ... the unmodishness of his 'poetry of the heart' in the avant-garde atmosphere of the early twenties. He looses his own shafts at the ... conceptualistic, the self-propagating and self-sufficing 'creationist', poetics manners that in his view draw on more previously elaborated art than on life.[16]

What 'Poetry' articulates most clearly is Paterson's championing of this aesthetic. 'If feeling yields a steadier light', the poem continues, 'then the poet knows / the pure verse, when it finally comes, / will sound like a mountain spring'. Here, the turn in the sonnet can be seen to focus on the crux of what, for Paterson, Machado's brand of poetic authenticity is really about: the only warranted intensity in the poem is that of the original emotion that fired it, which remains its fundamental raison d'être. But in order for it to truly resonate, this emotion needs to be tempered. The metaphorical comparison with the diamond at the start of the poem turns out to be especially apposite in this regard: it is only with the polish and serendipitous craft of poetic form that such poetry can take shape. This picks up on Paterson's interest in the challenges of poetic form. Freed from conscious thought, form can help enable the poet to kindle the kind of intellectually and emotionally transformative effects that Paterson especially values, more readily allowing language and the unconscious to take the reins of the poem, as opposed to the more manipulative and often predictable machinations of the conscious mind. But beyond this, 'Poetry' also advocates a kind of transcendent lyricism, in which the personal is given over to the anonymous: not in pursuit of artistic authority, as such, but to enable thought and feeling to be more fully infused.

'Beneath the blue oblivious sky, the water / sings of nothing, not your name, not mine', concludes the final couplet of 'Poetry', burning away any authorial command in favour of another image of transparent clarity. The blue sky, like the mountain spring, like the flow of water, sings only of absence – an absence perhaps best understood as a correlative to the Buddhist concept of *śūnyatā*, the Sanskrit for 'emptiness' or 'voidness', itself referring to enlightenment as a world 'empty of a self, or of anything pertaining to a self'.[17] Ultimately, Paterson's adaptation of Machado here confirms what Michael Wood surmises of the Spanish poet: 'Machado is a great lyric poet who is also thinking, even when he seems not to be – he has managed never to hear of T. S. Eliot's famous dissociation of sensibility ... or if he has heard of it, he works through it, and denies it.'[18] As we shall see, it is Paterson's desire to do exactly that for his own poetry: questioning, revaluating, and extending the intellectual and emotional range of his own verse under the influence of Machado, his lyric ally.

Just as Machado seems to have enabled Paterson to embrace more thoroughly anonymous and adaptable modes of address than Eliot's self-abnegating impersonality, the Spanish poet's example also proves inspirational in Paterson's increasing interest in overcoming the divisive line between thought and feeling in verse. This 'dissociation of sensibility', first outlined by Eliot in his famous essay 'The Metaphysical Poets', offers a convincing argument for a divide between erudition and emotion that, in Eliot's view, developed during the poetry of the seventeenth century:

> The difference is not a simple difference of degree between poets ... it is the difference between the intellectual poet and the reflective poet. Tennyson and Browning are poets, and they think; but they do not feel their thought as immediately as the odour of a rose. A thought to Donne was an experience; it modified his sensibility. When a poet's mind is perfectly equipped for its work, it is constantly amalgamating disparate experience; the ordinary man's experience is chaotic, irregular, fragmentary. The latter falls in love, or reads Spinoza, and these two experiences have nothing to do with each other ... in the mind of the poet these experiences are always forming new wholes. We may express the difference by the following theory: the poets of the seventeenth century, the successors of the dramatists of the sixteenth, possessed a mechanism of sensibility which could devour any kind of experience. In the seventeenth century a dissociation of sensibility set in, from which we have never recovered.[19]

In the previous chapter, discussion of poems such as 'Imperial' and 'Prologue' showed Paterson to be stylistically close to

Donne in this manner, intellectualising the amorous in the former piece, and combining sceptical rigour with impassioned resolve in matters spiritual in the latter. In *The Eyes*, Machado's influence enables this project to develop in earnest, without the cover of overtly self-deprecating irony that pervades *God's Gift to Women*. As McKendrick notes, Machado's poetry not only gives Paterson 'license to paint with a broader brush', but it is as if 'the disguise of Machado's voice has helped Paterson to broach the larger questions about existence less obliquely and with more emotional candour'.[20]

'The Eyes', the title poem of the volume, explores this dilemma of how to conduct oneself with both thought and feeling – of how to live a life in which, as Yeats put it, the rational 'business of the head in the world is to bow a ceaseless obeisance to the heart', or, as Eliot noted of the Metaphysicals, to allow one's 'mode of feeling to be directly and freshly altered by … reading and thought'.[21] It tells the tale of a widower who decides, after his lover dies, to 'shut himself' away, alone with his memories of her and 'the big sunny mirror / where she'd fix her hair' (*SP* 60). In a fashion not dissimilar to the drunken speaker in *God's Gift to Women*'s 'A Private Bottling' (*SP* 33), proposing a toast to 'your sweet memory, but not to you', the widower in 'The Eyes' hopes that his beloved might remain 'intact', if only he can preserve the pureness of her painfully permanent absence. Paterson picks up on Machado's original by likening this act to a 'great block of gold / he hoarded like a miser', the suggestion being that while art and memory may afford a momentary stay against time's passing (indeed, Machado once famously described poetry as 'la palabra en el tiempo', which is to say 'the word in time', or as Robert Bly puts it, 'human language in which we feel time passing'[22]), any attempt to permanently halt its linear arrow is doomed to grief and loneliness. So it proves for the widower who, 'around the first anniversary', begins to wonder what colour his lover's eyes were. But his reflections in solitude fail to yield more than panic: '*Were they brown or black, / or grey? Green? Christ! I can't say …*' (*SP* 60).

The poem argues that the vagaries of personal memory, like the fleeting reflections of a mirror, fail to preserve the past. It is, rather, a chance encounter of a purely visual nature that can deliver the truth, in the here-and-now of time's flow, as 'one

Spring morning, something gave in him': the widower 'shut the front door, turned into the street' and in a moment 'from a dark close, / he caught a flash of eyes'. The past is thus defined and sustained by the present and the future – a continuum in which time, as Paterson puts it in 'Marginal Notes' (a short sequence elsewhere in *The Eyes* that picks up on Machado's *ars poetica*), is a 'clear stream', and genuine poetry the 'lyric grammar / where today is tomorrow, yesterday, still' (*TE* 15–16). In turn, it appears the way to link them is to see clearly, to combine thought with feeling, to study the outer world without losing the depths of the inner world. As Bly puts it in a manner especially pertinent to 'The Eyes': 'If we look only at our problems, Machado said, the inner world dissolves; if we look only at the world, it begins to dissolve. If we want to create art, we have to stitch together the inner and the outer world. How to do that? Machado concludes, well, we could always use our eyes.'[23]

In the end, the widower in the poem does exactly that, but whether this act of seeing 'brings home the truth quite uncomplicatedly', as Trueblood argues, is another matter. In his translation of this particular Machado piece, Trueblood's speaker emphatically concludes that the eyes he encounters are the very image of his lover's: 'Like those!'[24] But in Paterson's poem, the widower seems neither fully sure nor convinced. 'He lowered his hat-brim / and walked on ... *yes, they were like that; like that ...*' (*SP* 60). The moment of clear-eyed perception, a vivid encounter with the here-and-now, delivers some reassurance, but it is by no means obvious that it delivers convincing truth.

Paterson's version of Machado does not so readily meet with the Spanish poet's belief in the 'act of seeing' as might initially seem the case. On the one hand, of course, 'The Eyes' (and *The Eyes* more generally) does find Paterson reiterating Machado's attempts to combine the philosophical force of intuitive thought with the sensory abundance and genuine immediacy of feeling. 'Paterson is keen to put culture in its place', as William Scammell quips in a review of *The Eyes*, 'that is, back in the ordinary human heart'.[25] We might also refer to the way in which the perceived duality of thought and feeling complements Paterson's allegiance to a poetic understanding of the monistic state of the world, expressed in an early poem such as 'The Ferryman's

Arms'. But on the other hand, the closing lines of 'The Eyes' are not fully compatible with Machado's assertion that 'only vision is evidence, and that one never doubts what one sees, only what one thinks'.[26] For Paterson, the act of seeing is always ripe for questioning, and part of the perceptually restricted nature of human consciousness, 'the human dream', that is an increasingly central concern in his poetry. While Paterson does find a powerful kinship with what Trueblood describes as Machado's 'prolonged effort to reconcile an inborn lyric impulse with a conceptualising bent of mind',[27] it is a more heightened awareness, or perhaps simply wariness, of the raw qualia of experience that will separate Paterson from Machado, in his blending of thought and feeling in poetry.

If a natural combination of philosophical thought and genuine feeling were readily apparent in any of Paterson's poems before he explicitly took up the example of Machado, 'A Private Bottling' is likely the most memorable example (*SP* 33). This meditatively confessional lyric in *God's Gift to Women*, structured around the speaker's long night of whisky sampling, appears to be as much about the drunken exorcism of a former lover as it is 'shy negotiations' with matters spiritual. In particular, the poem illustrates Paterson's development of his own twist on the *via negativa*, in searching for spiritual meaning and an abiding loving faith without a godhead, one that can sit comfortably alongside his sceptical, philosophically rigorous and increasingly scientific-materialist outlook. For a poet wanting to combine an openly intuitive frame of mind with intellectual rigour, negative transcendence through poetic language offers an attractive solution.

In his version of a sonnet from Machado's series of 'Parábolas' ('Parables'), Paterson formulates this credo with greater conviction and clarity. In doing so, however, he is also careful in attempts not to sacrifice the necessary obliquity that negative affirmation requires. As such, 'Profession of Faith' begins in much the same manner as Machado's original, presenting the extended conceit of the sea as a representation of God – or rather, suggesting how the sea's features bear comparison with His fluid omnipresence. 'He scatters like the moonlight on the water / or appears on the horizon like a sail', the poem claims, delivering one intense image that illustrates the deity's brilliant but fleeting appearance, before another demonstrates God's unexpected, distant, and typically intangible nature (*SP* 61).

What follows is perhaps the most intellectually demanding aspect of the poem, and a prime example of what Trueblood means when he says that 'the enigmas and obscurities of Machado's poetry are neither obscurantist or wilful'.[28] Rather, as Paterson clearly admires and succeeds in reimagining on his own terms, they emerge from the effort to confront fundamental questions about, and complex paradoxes inherent to, the human condition. As Paterson has stated in interview, when asked about the issue of 'accessibility' in poetry: 'I think it's possible to write of things of immense philosophical subtlety in a language readers can follow. But I do understand that the stranger, more complex and more difficult the idea, the greater your obligation to clear expression.'[29] So 'Profession of Faith' continues:

> He made the sea, and like the clouds and storms
> is born of it, over and over. Thus the Creator
> finds himself revived by his own creature:
> he thrives on the same spirit he exhales. (*SP* 61)

Indeed, these lines do manage to capture a complex, abstract idea in language that feels unadorned and clear, albeit musically attuned. According to the poem, God is best understood as an omnipresence forever at one with everything, sustained by the very world he has created, 'born of it, over and over'. In other words, He is not to be conceived of as a distinct being, but one dissolved into symbiotic union with His creation, the world: in fact, the last line of the above excerpt is rendered in Trueblood's more faithful translation of Machado's original as 'his breath is spirit, and by the spirit he breathes'.[30] For Paterson, the appeal of such a concept seems clear enough: if we conceive of God as essentially at one with the flow of creation, then a spiritually open understanding of the world from an inherently matter-based, broadly scientific perspective, without need for a godhead, is not just possible but is also philosophically justified.

With this metaphysical thesis in place inside the first eight lines of the poem, it is unsurprising to find Paterson separating out the fourteen lines of Machado's sonnet into octave and a concluding, more emotionally eloquent sestet. The turn that follows in 'Profession of Faith' not only makes an emphatic vow to this new, material-bound Lord to 'uncover / your name in my own', but also to 'restore / the soul you gifted me'. In the previous chapter, discussion was made of the way in which Paterson had wrestled with his dismissal of God, and 'his vast retinue of fairies and pixies' that were 'considerably more difficult to kill off', while also wanting to retain a spiritual cast of mind (*O* 65). In 'Profession of Faith', an anonymously voiced, philosophically explorative approach allows for the realisation that if the spiritual can reside in the ebb and flow of corporeal existence, then a view of the soul as something 'bred' from matter can be both legitimately argued and sustained. And it is this knowledge, as Paterson has claimed in interview, that frees us, with poetry's guidance, from the notion 'of a truth we can't directly access, but which exists in the hands of some remote and inscrutable third party, and which we have to guess at. Poetry shows us as freelance truth-improvisers ... it restores our human independence a little.'[31]

Machado's example variously enables the development and refinement of Paterson's poetic practice. *The Eyes* not only illustrates Paterson's ability to craft increasingly self-sufficient poems that combine thought with annealed emotion, adopting an anonymous poetic voice that attempts to articulate communal feelings beyond the merely solipsistic. It also finds him developing original solutions to the tension between his sharply philosophical, sceptical bent of mind and the counterbalancing godless spiritualism he refuses to relinquish. 'Siesta', the final poem from *God's Gift to Women* that heralded the beginning of the Machado project, reappears in *The Eyes* to assert its importance and centrality in Paterson's poetic thinking, and his by now fully fledged commitment to poetry as a mode of knowledge. At the close of his 'Afterword' to *The Eyes*, Paterson acknowledges, beyond Machado, the 'tutelary voice' and 'hand in the dark' of Emil Cioran (*TE* 60), an aphorist whose refined brand of philosophical scepticism Paterson has elsewhere described as 'a kind of terrible, insomniac enlightenment. To read him openly as a Westerner is thus to be a little *reprogrammed*' (*TBS* 195). As was discussed in the prologue, this is precisely what Paterson espouses as the 'true' aim of poetry: 'risk', as he defines it in his *ars poetica* essay 'The Dark Art of Poetry', is that which 'makes readers feel genuinely uncomfortable, excited, open to suggestion, vulnerable to reprogramming, complicit in the creative business of their transformation'.[32] It is Cioran, perhaps as much as Machado, who gives Paterson the nerve to subscribe to both the composition and reading of poetry as a unique mode of thinking. 'Much more than in the school of philosophers', Cioran once claimed, 'it is in the academy of the poets that we learn the courage of intelligence and the audacity to be ourselves'.[33]

Opening on a scene during the eponymous drowsy midday hour, 'Siesta' depicts a still and formal garden where the only perceptible movements are a 'fire-fish' swimming in a pool, above which the stone statue of a cherub in flight is suspended, and the 'poem' of the cicada, fluttering and 'ringing hollow in the elm'. 'Let us praise the Lord', announces the poem's speaker, 'who has declared / this silence in the pandemonium' (*SP* 74). For a moment, Paterson here quotes Machado's original phrasing near-exactly, as he allows the poem to openly relish the possibility of a God, as conceived in 'Profession of Faith', who is no more or less than the flow of the universe's matter. Paterson's poem is thus in part a tribute to a God who, in some ways, isn't a god at all, but a broadly spiritual guarantor of the wonder of the universe, of understanding and 'pandemonium' that exists beyond the perceptual limitations and cognitive mechanisms of the human mind: 'the God of absence and of aftermath, / of the anchor in the sea', that 'brimming sea' that represents the flux and complexity of the universe, while also recalling the self-same metaphor for God that was conjured in 'Profession of Faith'.

But 'Siesta' is also a tribute to absence and negation themselves, as those which secure the possibility of engaged human thought in the first instance. It is this 'truant omnipresence', as it were, that 'sets us free / from this world' of objects, sensations, and phenomena, onto what Paterson claims, more fervently than either Trueblood or Bly's more faithful translations of Machado's original, is 'the one true path'. Machado's belief, as Trueblood summarises it, is that 'by looking hard enough the poet will be able to see into things, see through and beyond them … and in the process grasp the nature of their reality and what lies beyond it'.[34] For Paterson, as we shall find in our discussion of *Landing Light* in the following chapter, this concept becomes the raison d'être for his poetic composition, as an attuned awareness of 'the human dream' encourages thinking, and in turn poetry, of ever bolder philosophical speculation:

> When the object is allowed to shrug off its name, it begins the long road back to its own intrinsic mystery – and on finally reaching the core of its own estranging fire, radiates until the whole world is unified by it. The paperclip or the rose; either could open the path back to our awakening. (*TBS* 13)

A number of Machado's later poems, 'Siesta' included, were attributed to the invented noms de plume of Abel Martín and Juan de Mairena. These 'expressive outlets', as Trueblood puts it, were 'geared to the increasing complexity and subtlety of his mature thinking', as well as figuring as a guard, no doubt, against Machado's own sense of insufficient qualification as a philosopher.[35] But if we take Michael Wood's suggestion that 'in any liberated form of translation' such as Paterson's versioning of Machado 'the translated writer can seem a kind of fiction, a shadowy ancestor haunting the dream prehistory of the work',[36] then, for Paterson, Machado can be seen to serve as that very figure himself. In taking the example of, and cues from, Machado, while also partly sheltering under the guise of this unapologetically earnest, intellectually and emotionally challenging Spanish poet, Paterson has been able to create new poems of his own that are more than just artistic portraiture, but that have freed him to fully voice and expound ideas, feelings, and concepts that he previously approached only with tentative irony, or else evaded. In this way, *The Eyes* lays the stylistic and thematic groundwork for the poems of Paterson's fourth volume, *Landing Light*, where the following aphorism of Machado's might be seen as the guiding beams on the runway of Paterson's poetic imagination:

> We are victims, I thought, of a double hallucination. If we look outward, and concentrate on entering things, our external world begins to lose solidity, and if we conclude that it exists not in and for itself, but exists because of us, it ends by dissolving. However, if, moved by our private reality, we turn our eyes inward, then the world pushes in on us, and it is our interior world, our being, that disappears. What to do then? Weave the thread given to us, dream our dream and live; it is the only way we can achieve the miracle of growth.[37]

4

Shrewd Obliquity of Speech:
Landing Light (2003)

While *The Eyes* marked an undeniable departure in Paterson's poetry, allowing him to embrace and assimilate Machado's earnestness, philosophical seriousness, and emotional candour, it could also be argued that, as a collection of poems that repeatedly takes its points of departure from the Spanish poet, it nevertheless remains to read as a project, rather than an achievement in the fullest sense. *Landing Light*, Paterson's fourth volume, represents a more substantial development and achievement. 'It is only 10 years since Don Paterson's much welcomed debut *Nil Nil*', states Bernard O'Donoghue in a review of the collection, 'but in the course of that decade he has become a major presence. The qualities for which his early poems were praised – hard-edged wit and technical brilliance – have remained in evidence, but his poetry has increasingly added to these skills a seriousness and moral urgency.'[1] As Sean O'Brien notes, 'here, it seems, after the intriguing samples and trailers, is what Paterson, *mezzo del cammin*, can *actually do*'.[2]

Our previous discussion of an early poem from *Nil Nil*, 'An Elliptical Stylus', revealed the manner in which, as Sarah Broom suggests, 'Paterson's characteristic approach is to grab the individual reader by the collar and insist upon the idea of the poem as a personal exchange between poet-speaker and actual individual reader'.[3] Paterson tends to make use of direct address in his poems as a means of insisting on the reader's attentive and active engagement with the poem as a serious piece of intellectual discourse, however entertaining it might prove. As Natalie Pollard states, in discussing the intricate associations between Paterson's poet-speakers and his audience, 'for Paterson, the really valuable poem builds not on passive complaisance but complexity and challenge in its publicly inflected "special relationship" with readers'.[4]

In *Landing Light*, Paterson's understanding of the complexity of the relationship between poem, poet-speaker, and audience is extended to greater depths. A typical Paterson poem is often extremely conscious of itself, and by extension all poetry, as necessary fiction, a work of constructed artifice. But, as Adam Newey has argued, Paterson nonetheless manages to avoid being 'trapped by his intellectual labyrinths'. 'The effect', Newey suggests, 'is to triangulate the position of the self from its relationship to others'.[5] As Pollard states: 'Paterson's poems invite their readers into intimate exchange-relations with poets and readers across the ages.'[6] But the question remains as to how they succeed in doing so.

The linguistic concept of deixis is an illuminating way of understanding the time-shifting and -conflating abilities of Paterson's verse. In his paper 'Deixis and the Poetic Persona', Keith Green defines deixis as 'the encoding in an utterance of the spatio-temporal context and subjective experience of the encoder'.[7] In any utterance, he suggests, there is the relation of the speaker's 'centre' and a 'surrounding cognitive environment'; but, in poetry, because of the absence of extralinguistic elements, 'actual situation and emotional situation will be compounded'.[8] Poems work under the assumption of an addressee and a decoder, and poets who are especially aware of this arrangement can dramatise and exploit this, manipulating the different time frames that may co-exist in the poem: the time frame of the poet as author, the time frame of the historical persona and addressee(s), the here-and-now time frame of the poem as it is experienced by the reader. As Green claims: 'Language seems to be designed primarily for face-to-face interaction (that is, the canonical situation of the utterance); but it is a capability of humans that they can mobilise discourse beyond this canonical situation and operate language free of contextual boundaries.'[9] Poetry is a pertinent, complex, and unique example of this.

Perhaps more than any other poem in *Landing Light*, 'The Reading' finds Paterson utilising poetic deixis and direct address to the reader. The poem does so to self-reflexively illustrate the shifting, context-warping interactions that lyric poems variously depend upon – between poet-speaker, addressee, and audience. It opens with attention-grabbing lines that meet the reader *in medias res*, and draw us in with the intimacy of their address:

> The first time I came to your wandering attention
> my name was Simonides. Poets,
> whose air of ingratitude forms in the womb,
> have reason at least to thank me:
> I invented the thing you now call the commission.
> Oh – and one other frivolity
> refined by Aquinas, tuned up by Bruno
> and perfected by Hannibal Lecter. (*SP* 99)

This opening stanza does a surprising amount of work in setting the poem's complex scenario, character, and tone. The first two lines invoke a speaker and an audience that encompasses both individual reader and assumed poet-speaker, drawing on the time frame of the here-and-now reception of the poem as it is being read, as well as the prior moment of authorly composition. But at the same time, they also gesture towards an author and an audience across time, in harking back to Simonides of Ceos, the ancient Greek lyric poet, who is, we are told, the 'first' incarnation of the current poem's fluid speaker. This poet is the one who comes to your 'wandering attention' – the attention, that is, of the shifting audience through time that a poem must meet, entertain, and convince, in order to secure its posterity. 'In reading Paterson, one is accosted by the diverse ways in which the poem ... articulates the fraught relationships between personal and social, private and public', notes Pollard.[10] In 'The Reading', this dynamic is exposed and dissected, extending Paterson's earlier appreciation of Machado's example, in attempting to produce poems that resonate both inside and outside of the self and of time, through a combination of immediacy and enduring memorability.

Unlike the wholly philosophical and aesthetically minded poems of *The Eyes*, however, in 'The Reading' the commercial aspect of lyric poetry – what Pollard describes as the way in which 'lyric success depends on making canny socio-economic moves in front of listening bodies'[11] – makes plain the interrelation of poetry and trade. 'I invented the thing you now call the commission', boasts the poet-speaker, suggesting that ungrateful poets should be thankful for the money-making opportunities he has afforded them. But to read such a statement baldly would be to ignore how 'The Reading' implies that the semblance of financial stability offered in the form of commissioned work – be it as part of the ancient patronage system, or in terms of modern requests from organisations and arts-funding bodies – is one of the few securities available to the lyric poet in the face of poetry audiences' capricious interests. What of that 'other frivolity' the poet-speaker cryptically alludes to? 'All in good time', we are told, a canny move to intrigue and keep the audience's attention, exemplifying what Michael Donaghy has called a poem's 'social transaction ... the give and take between artist and participating audience in an oral tradition'.[12]

'But first to the theme / of this evening's address: the reading', Paterson's poem continues in its crafted extempore (*SP* 99). The remainder of 'The Reading' forms a parable of sorts, refashioning an apocryphal ancient Greek tale concerning Simonides, in which the poet gives a reading of his work for a 'little king' at a feast held in a great hall. The fluid and anonymous poet-speaker in Paterson's poem recounts how this performance included a commissioned poem, supposed to honour the dubious king – 'not a good poem, if I say so myself' – that contained so many references to Castor and Pollux, the mythical twin sons of Leda ('I ended up fleshing it out, as you do, / with something I'd found in the drawer'), that the disgruntled patron offers 'only one-half the struck price'. This led the indignant poet to show his anger, we are told, which only served to leave him floundering in a disapproving silence, 'at which point / I thought it a smart move to drop it' (*SP* 100). However:

> I fixed each man's face in my mind,
> each man at his rank at the table
> (that trick of mine; your coupons, O my rapt listeners,
> I'll have nailed by the end of this poem). (*SP* 100)

These four lines, falling in the centre of the poem, are crucial to its argument. They announce the earlier 'frivolity' the poet-speaker made a cryptic reference to – his inventive ability to visually memorise a scene using the mnemonic device of the method of loci, otherwise known as the 'memory palace', in which spatial visualisation allows discrete content to be ordered and successfully recalled. The persuasive memorability of a poem through its musical and semantic cohesion is a feature on which Paterson places a particularly high value. In his treatise *The Poem: Lyric, Sign, Metre*, he goes so far as to argue that it is part of poetry's raison d'être – especially in its original, mimetic form. Echoing sentiments explored and evinced in the Machadian poems of *The Eyes*, poetry, he suggests, 'has always been an "aspirant" form, one which seeks to transcend human limitations of memory. For a long time it seems it was an art barely distinguishable from song. However, poetry retained a unique and near-magical property. It is the one art form where its memory and its acquisition are one and the same thing.'[13]

Here, Paterson is also making indirect reference to the bardic tradition of poetry, in which poets served a specific function in pre-historical communities, making use of poetry's mnemonic devices – assonance, alliteration, rhyme, and so on – to commit intricate oral histories to the collective tribal memory. As well as being an entertaining yarn about the vagaries of the poet's life, and the complex relationship between poet, poem, and audience that plays out in intimate, public, and commercial fashion across time, 'The Reading' also argues for the power and authority poets once wielded, and may still do, in telling you something that you will never forget. But there is muted anger and aggression in the above-quoted lines, too, in the eloquent phrasings of Paterson's direct address to the reader. Paterson's approach can often be steely eyed, insistent, and even threatening. As Peter Howarth states, his narrators make 'every would-be casual reader into a sparring partner'.[14] The 'coupons' that the poet-speaker sinisterly promises to have 'nailed' by the end of the poem might seem a merely metaphorical suggestion – like a detachable coupon, the poet's visualising memory trick will, however disquietingly, simply allow him to keep a record of his readers. But as well as the aggressive connotations of the verb 'nailed', if we consider that the Latinate etymology of 'coupon' is *colaphus,* meaning 'a blow with the fist', the poet's promise takes on the feel of a more directly physical threat.

What was assuring in the direct address at the beginning of the poem here becomes rather disconcerting – even more so when read in the light of 'the end of this poem'. As we discover, the gods are angered on behalf of Simonides and consequently bring down, with a Zeus-like 'great thunderbolt', the hall roof 'on the lot of them'. Just as Simonides was the only one able to identify the 'disfigured' and 'tenderised menfolk' for the grieving wives ('*And the hawknose? / Poor woman: look under your feet*'; (*SP* 101)), the poem forces us to question how the poet-speaker will have similarly 'nailed' our faces by its close, and to consider how poets and poems 'read' us as much as we read them. In the final instance, 'The Reading' is as much about the beguiling and complex technique of direct address, in which poets ensure that their paying audience are suitably engaged and so stay with them, as it is about the canny and manipulative means that this selfsame approach can serve. In wielding power over said readers, the poem's direct address ensures that the historically enshrined importance of poetry is not underestimated, or dismissed as mere entertainment. As the 'fixed gaze' of the dead patron is held by the poet while he 'knelt in the rafters and carefully counted / the rest of my fee from his purse', 'The Reading' implies that while readers are mortal and come and go, the successful poem, and by extension its speaker, enjoys an immortality through its perennially fresh, immediate mode of address to new audiences, manipulating poetic deixis so as to always ensure that an appropriate 'fee' is extracted.

Throughout Paterson's oeuvre, the theme of dividedness – whether it be truthful paradoxes lurking beneath the seeming contradiction of conventional opposites, or the unitary illusion of the self – is an abiding fascination and source of broader intellectual enquiry. 'The self is a universal vanishing point' (*BE* 51) he claims in one aphorism, as well as noting with a certain seriocomic intent: 'No, I'm not obsessed with myself, just *the* self; I could be just as easily mesmerised by yours, if it were as readily available for study' (*BE* 22).

In *Landing Light*, this concept of the divided identity, and particularly the trope of the doppelgänger, is extended to the level of Gothic obsession, in which it finds its origins. Writing in *The Gothic Other*, Ruth Bienstock Anolik outlines the Gothic as a literary genre 'marked by an anxious encounter with otherness, a dark and mysterious unknown'.[15] She goes on to suggest that the nature of the Gothic veers towards 'representing the fearful unknown as the inhuman Other: the supernatural or monstrous manifestation ... that symbolises all that is irrational, uncontrollable and incomprehensible'. But if all this gives the impression that the disturbing force of the Other is bound to a primitive sense of the evil and supernatural, and can be dismissed in the wake of the Enlightenment and the birth of modern science, the Gothic literary imagination of the late eighteenth century and nineteenth illustrates the abiding purpose and value of such fear: what the Other can tell us about ourselves, and how it will always 'relocate to new dark spaces'.[16] We might be in possession of a modern, rational self that thinks it has debunked such fears as the product of irrationality, adopting scientific accounts of the world as a kind of dogma – one that ensures, as Alison Milbank has memorably put it, that the mind 'remains emperor of its own experience'.[17] But this 'modern, buffered self', as Milbank also argues, is exactly 'the subjectivity the Gothic tale of the doppelgänger seeks to question, showing that the buffers do not work'.

It is not difficult to see how these ideas map onto Paterson's poetic credo. The concept of the 'buffered' self, coined by Charles Taylor in his volume *A Secular Age*, and with which Milbank sees the Gothic literary imagination in battle, is in many ways similar to what Paterson conceives of as 'the human dream'. Both gesture towards our near-constant state of anthropocentric arrogance, fostered by our tendency to see everything in terms of its human use and purpose. As we will later discuss, Paterson's poems evince a growing belief that poetry is best equipped to transcend this delimiting state of mind, so that the world and its objects are 'redreamt, they are reimagined, they are remade', and so 'repossess something of their mystery, their infinite possibility'.[18] But first, it is valuable for us to consider how the poems in *Landing Light* make specific use of the Gothic doppelgänger trope, and how, in turn, they reveal anxieties and fears about the nature of the self, art, and poetic composition.

Whereas a poem such as 'The Hunt' (*SP* 91) concerns a poet-speaker who comes to recognise the divided nature of his self – his art enacting a constant tussle between the conventional rationality of his waking mind, and the shadowy 'Other' of his disturbing subconscious – a companion poem, 'A Fraud' (*SP* 97), acts out a quasi-confession of an apparently more deliberate doubling. With its alternately rhymed quatrains in tight metrical form, the poem adopts similar strictures to 'The Hunt', though it begins with a much more conventional quotidian scene. The young poet-speaker is innocently 'crossing / a field near Bridgefoot', we are told, when his eye happens to catch 'something glossing / the toe of his boot' (*SP* 97). On closer inspection, this reveals itself as a 'tiny wellhead' in the rock that, in typical Patersonian fashion, takes on supernatural characteristics as the narrative begins to segue into the strange, 'straining through the gap / as a little clear tongue / that replenished its shape / by the shape of its song'. The appearance of this tiny fountain has a fairytale-like quality to it – indeed, the folkloric quality of this and other poems in *Landing Light* can be traced back to Paterson's earlier work. The appeal, as ever, is the perceptually transformative possibilities such a tradition allows for, in segueing between the familiar and the uncanny. In 'A Fraud', as elsewhere, this is something that should serve to put us on our guard, not least when the wellhead begins to talk:

> It said *Son*
> *I've no business with you.*
> *Whatever I own*
> *is the next fellow's due.*
>
> *But if I'm his doom*
> *or Castalian spring –*
> *your directive's the same:*
> *keep walking.* (SP 97)

As the poet-speaker goes on to confess, he couldn't resist the temptation. The promise of this peculiar wellhead offering itself up as a Castalian spring – the mythologised source of Ancient Greek poetic inspiration that lies in the valley beside Mount Parnassus, the legendary home of the Muses – was enough to make him 'drop like a hawk', and 'swallow its shout / in the cave of his breast'. 'Now two strangers shiver / under one roof', he resignedly tells us: one who is the rational self, issuing 'the promise' and 'proof', and the other who is the stolen poetic talent, deployed 'for the poem or the kiss' (*SP* 98).

In spite of this, the poem's ostensible confession cannot be a straightforward admission of theft, since its fantastical fairytale is so clearly one of allegorical significance. Rather, the poem makes a particular show of inviting us to *read in*, and unpick the deeper significance of the figurative storyline it weaves. As Paterson argues in his *ars poetica*:

> Poetry is as much a mode of reading as writing. The reader must know they are reading a poem to read-it-as-a-poem, and apply all the human powers of signification and connection the poem asks of them. (Some of the most artful poems have the habit of disguising themselves as far simpler statements than they really are; any reader who isn't reading such a poem in an oversignifying mode will most likely miss the best of it.)[19]

The suggestion here is that all poems depend upon the reader's understanding of poetry as a genre that requires them to 'read between the lines'. A poem manipulates language's tendency to oversignify, but in order for it to succeed, this has to operate in conjunction with the human capacity to make imaginative connections and meaning. We are back to the concept of the poem as a conversation, or even an 'act of collusion', as Paterson has elsewhere suggested.[20]

In 'A Fraud', the first such invitation for us to *read in* appears in the poem's repeated use of images of water and fountains. On one level, we might interpret the 'tiny wellhead' that the poet-speaker encounters as a parody of traditional ideas of poetic 'sources' of inspiration. Paterson's practice and critical writing can often evince a belief in true poetry as arriving, in part, from an unconscious source. But in his concomitant commitment to craft and the painstaking apprenticeship of the poet, Paterson appears to reject Romantic ideals of the Muse, and other sources of 'inspiration' from without. The speaking wellhead in 'A Fraud' is thus a deliberately farcical construct, the embodiment of what Paterson suggests are outmoded notions of poetic origin – 'the Castalian spring' itself being the origin of all such myths. But, on another level, the fact that the poem communicates the poet-speaker's unshakeable sense that he has somehow stolen his own talent, in turn lends weight to the persistent truth of the poet's disconnection from his bardic abilities. The poem arises from within rather than without, as the poet-speaker suggests, yet still he feels detached and divided, as if another self, a stranger, is 'deployed / for the poem' (*SP* 98). In this way, 'A Fraud' speaks of the anxiety that the peculiar and mysterious process of poetic composition engenders, and by extension, asks us as readers the more broadly significant question of what authenticity amounts to. The poet may understand that his negotiations with what Michael Donaghy calls the 'resistant medium'[21] of poetic form are what enable his unconscious to come to the fore, giving rise to the illusion of poetic 'inspiration' from without; but the intuitive feeling of the poet, of 'two strangers' that 'shiver / under one roof', still seems to confirm this illusion as true. The battle, it seems, is between the ego and the poem – the ego that wants to own the poem, and the poem that only emerges unbidden, and of its own mysterious accord, 'where a tiny wellhead / had broken the rock'. As Paterson notes in his self-reflective critical essay 'The Dilemma of the Peot [sic]': 'While it's fine for the ego to *drive* you to the gig, God help you if it's the ego that's up on stage.'[22]

As such, 'A Fraud' is also in dialogue with some of the key ideas that we saw Paterson develop in *The Eyes*, through Machado's tutelary example. As we found in critical analysis of the manifesto-in-miniature 'Poetry' in the previous chapter, Paterson adopts Machado's line in advocating a kind of transcendental lyricism as the ideal, in which the personal is given over to the anonymous, as the original emotion that fired the poem is tempered by deeply philosophical reflection. Images of flowing water abound in the Machadian versions of *The Eyes*, as a symbol of manifest truth and the pursuit of truth: recall how 'Poetry' invokes the 'pure verse' as sounding like 'a mountain spring, anonymous and serene' (*SP* 71), while 'Song' maps onto the imagery of 'A Fraud' even more closely, with its instruction to listen for 'the water in the rock' (*TE* 46). With all this in mind, it might be said that, for Paterson, the all-too-human self-centredness of the poet is often the obstacle to the poem, and the most problematic part of the process. 'An algorithm for poetry would be incredibly complex, but not infinitely so', notes Paterson in *The Poem*, 'and its detachment from such catastrophically overvalued, sentimental constructs as "the individual voice" could be just the thing to see the cultural return of *anon.*, or even propel us into a new era of Classicism, should we desire or require such things'.[23] But in spite of this highly speculative suggestion that we might one day dispense with the poet altogether, Paterson's is a flawed, keenly felt, and – for all its unblinking frankness – humane poetry, that refuses to abandon humanity even as it frequently despairs at what it is to be human. Paterson's line on the 'illusory' condition of being a poet smacks of modest overstatement: 'I might feel like a poet after the poems are written, but since I'm no longer writing them, I can't be; it's just self-congratulation', he once claimed.[24] But the manner in which such an apparently self-chastising approach attempts to place the poem before the poet, also serves to increase said poem's likelihood of achieving what we have previously outlined as Paterson's sense of poetry's raison d'être: to reach beyond the habitual, blinkered perspective of the subjective consciousness – which is to say, the human dream – in the hope of apprehending and appreciating the complex nature of reality.

In 'A Fraud', it is this moment of genuine poetic inspiration – what Alice Oswald calls the 'invisible' subject of the poem presenting itself, 'the one you can't choose, the one that writes itself'[25] – that fires the poet-speaker's feelings of being a thief, as he 'steals' the poem from his own subconscious in the process of its systematic interrogation. The 'two strangers' that make up the one self in 'A Fraud' are, in essence, the two sides necessary for poetic composition: the intellectually and artistically manipulative conscious mind, and the unbidden spontaneity and imagination of unrehearsed sensibility. The uneasiness that underpins this particular sense of a divided self is what primarily informs another poem in *Landing Light*, 'The Rat'.

The subject of this ingenious meta-poem is 'a poem about a rat' written by an anonymous 'young man' (*SP* 102). The poem is so good that the precocious talent's assumed literary elders, including the narrator, are amazed by and envious of it in equal measure. 'It was the best poem ever written about a rat', the poem's second line declares, creating an identical end-rhyme with the first line that serves to emphasise the dumbfounding brilliance the poem has had on the poet-speaker: 'To read it was to ask the rat to perch / on the arm of your chair until you turned the page' (*SP* 102). After stumbling on this seeming literary genius and finally extracting more poems from him, however, it turns out that the poem about a rat was something of a fluke, and the other work was 'not much good'. At which, the assumed jury of established poets take it upon themselves to offer him advice, about 'his tropes and turns, his metrical comportment', and instruct the young man to write more poems like The Rat. 'All we got was cheek from him. Then silence', the poet-speaker indignantly states: 'We gave up on him'. But the 'green arrogance' and 'one lucky strike' of the young writer of The Rat is one thing – the poem itself, quite another. When Paterson's poem shifts to the present day and the poet-speaker tells how 'today I read The Rat again', it is as good as he remembers, the young man's writing brimming with those two most valuable poetic qualities, at least as Paterson sees them: musical memorability, and the ability to conjure the illusion of the present moment. When combined, these seem to ensure The Rat's longevity, and sound a painful warning to the poet-speaker:

> Its reek
> announced it; then I saw its pisshole stare;
> line by line it strained into the air.
> Then it hissed. *For all the craft and clever-clever*
> *you did not write me, fool. Nor will you ever.* (SP 102)

The Rat's jeering prophecy to the poet-speaker is one that picks up on ideas discussed in 'A Fraud'. In his advice to the inexperienced young man who has penned The Rat, the literary elder is keen to offer advice on 'the wedding of the word to the event'. But the irony that Paterson knowingly conjures is that his own poem, 'The Rat', is no more than a poem *about* a poem called The Rat. It cannot succeed in pulling off the trick that the young man's poem does so effortlessly, making word and object appear as one and the same. For all the 'craft and clever-clever' – which is to say, for all the consciously manipulative and intelligent wordsmithery – ensures the good consistency of an experienced poet's writing, the truly excellent and unforgettable poem can still sometimes arrive, through freak alignment of individual imagination, time, place, circumstance, and so on, in the mind of a relative amateur. The Rat is thus the product of an unrehearsed sensibility, a lyric innocence and imagination that cannot be learnt or taught. While 'A Fraud' speaks of the anxiety created by the mysterious process of poetic composition, 'The Rat' gives a pertinent example of this in action: a poet who devotes their life to the craft and learning of poetry might never write a single poem that ranks alongside the 'one lucky strike' of an amateur.

As plainly humorous as the witty meta-poem of 'The Rat' is, it also probes further into the nature of the self – something that poems such as 'The Hunt' and 'A Fraud' suggest are the inevitable work of poetry, but that Paterson's poems achieve in ways that are both unusually frank and perceptive. Speaking in seriocomic fashion of the various life stages of the poet, Paterson has claimed that a poet's first life is that of 'lyric innocence', much as the young man in 'The Rat' exhibits – 'when they believe the word and its object to be perfectly interchangeable' (*TBS* 83). This is followed, apparently, by a second life in which they 'wake up to the fact that a poet is *someone whom words continually fail*'. It is then that he decides (and it is indeed described, perhaps in tellingly confessional fashion, as a 'he') to 'leave the tiny house of the poem to inspect the façade, and learn something of the architectural mysteries he once had no desire to penetrate' (*TBS* 84). It is this acute awareness of the problems of poetry as an art form, alongside its unique capacity to shed light on the complexities of the human condition, which informs *Landing Light*'s poems, especially those that evince some of Paterson's most complex poetic-philosophical thinking.

It is the principal underlying theme of Paterson's poetry that guarantees both his oeuvre's consistency and originality. The stylistic shifts from collection to collection, particularly the serious play with dramatis personae and the adoption of a more anonymised poetic voice, set Paterson apart from many of his contemporaries, especially those whose consistent poetic voice has become the hallmark of their uniqueness. But it is the purpose to which Paterson's stylistic arsenal is utilised that singles him out: namely, Paterson's increasing commitment to poetry as a powerful means of intellectual enquiry, one that might be ranked alongside science and philosophy in its unique ability to reimagine and remake our understanding of the world. In so many instances, the poetry's target and focal point is that of our habitually dulled, perceptually restricted human perspective. Which is to say that the poems look to interrogate – time and again and with increased sophistication and awareness – the false divide between our routine encounters with the

73

world, and the sense that the complex nature of reality lies beyond the boundaries of everyday perception.

'Poetry is the paradox of language turned against its own declared purpose', Paterson has claimed, 'that of nailing down the human dream'.[26] In the final poem of *Landing Light*, Paterson can be found attempting to articulate this poetic-philosophical thesis as a kind of all-encompassing treatise. 'I have never opened a book in my life, / made love to a woman, picked up a knife': so begins 'The White Lie', with a series of emphatic declarations that suggest themselves to be patently untrue (*SP* 114). 'Nor could I put a name to my own face', confesses the speaker, at which point we can be in no doubt, surely, that we have been lied to. But then, as the poem proposes, what *can* we say with any real authority that we 'know to be the case'? 'Everything ... draws its signal colour off the sight / till what falls into that intellectual night / we tunnel into this view or another'. By invoking the 'eye-beam' of ancient Greek understanding – the Aristotelian idea that a beam generated by the eye is responsible for sight – the poem offers up both a falsehood and a truth in the very same instance. For while modern science has long proven that the eye in fact receives rather than projects light, the outmoded Greek perspective of the eye-beam is not without its own figurative resonance. 'The light indeed pours from our eyes', writes Paterson in *The Blind Eye*, echoing the 'tunnel' vision proposed in 'The White Lie': 'its little, dim, narrow human light: we stand before the world like a projectionist behind his dusty cone of shadows, illuminating only what we already know' (*BE* 27).

Like 'The Ferryman's Arms' before it, 'The White Lie' is on one level a poem that finds Paterson engaging with the nature of perceptual paradox: what appears to be a falsehood, it suggests, can just as likely turn out to be a paradoxical truth. But where 'The Ferryman's Arms' ends on this note of brief perceptual awakening, its departing speaker leaving his other self 'stuck in his tent of light', 'The White Lie' takes this observation as its broader starting point. As such, the poem goes on to launch a poetic-philosophical enquiry into the nature of the human dream it proposes we inhabit, and how poetry might be able to expose, and even briefly transcend, this habitual state. The poem continues with a prayer: *'when I stand between the sunlit and the sun / make me glass'* (*SP* 114). Here, the speaker hopes to find a means of recovery from the distortive effects of consciousness on his perception. The solution proposed is a familiar one – in achieving a certain detached anonymity, the self becomes a kind of transparency. It should come as no surprise that the poem goes on to describe a sexual encounter, that at first recalls the spiritually redemptive, self-transcending qualities of genuine love and intimacy argued for in 'Letter to the Twins', in which the absent father of Romulus and Remus offers his sons tender advice on 'the honouring of your lover' (*SP* 95). Throughout Paterson's oeuvre, sexual intimacy often suggests itself as a possible means of spiritual enlightenment and redemption. As Edward Larrissy has noted of Paterson's love poetry: 'for Paterson, love is not merely sex: these poems attempt to describe the strangeness of the encounter with another, an encounter of which sexual discovery forms part'.[27] Yet, in spite of the poet in 'The White Lie' finding 'the girl look up at me and through / me with such a radiant wonder, you / could not read it as a compliment', in the end the moment of intimacy fails, and 'the light / stalled between us like a sheet, a door, a wall' (*SP* 114). Neither committed to the moment's subjective intensity nor capable of transcending it, the speaker can only offer a 'halfhearted opacity'.

'But consider this', the poem's speaker goes on to posit, in a direct address to the reader that announces renewed intent, a perspectival shift in the face of its prior account of apparently failed erotic transcendence. 'When we leave the room, / the chair, the bookend or the picture-frame / we had frozen by desire or spent desire / is reconsumed in its estranging fire'. Devoid of human presence, the objects of a room, the poem suggests, shrug off the imposition of their narrow human meaning. We might note also that the poem's invocation of fire as a catalytic image of 'estranging' imaginative rebirth echoes Paterson's use of the Promethean 'ashless blaze' in *The Eyes* (*SP* 72). In 'The White Lie' as in 'Promethean', fire figures as a means both of reigniting and of constantly shifting lifeless and delimiting perspectives. But while the 'room' in question may be the intimate theatre of the poet-speaker and his lover, it equally invokes the immediate and arresting presence of *this* room that you likely find yourself in right now, reading the poem. The poem's conjuring of the illusion of the present moment thus draws us into, and makes universal, its forceful philosophical argument. If we were to 'slip back' to this room 'too long asleep to feel our human tread' (*SP* 115) we might witness its objects anew, and in turn recognise that all things possess an abundance of possible meanings and functions beyond those imposed by the dead metaphors of human language.

The argument that 'The White Lie' puts forward illustrates how we are not passive receivers of an objectively verifiable reality ('the conducting element'), but rather 'the source' of all such meaning in the world, since we can't help but project our subjective reality into it. As such, the poem invites productive comparison with the radical aesthetic philosophy of Gilles Deleuze and Félix Guattari, particularly their concept of deterritorialisation. Broadly speaking, deterritorialisation is the decontextualising of a fixed set of relations between objects, ideas, or individuals, allowing them to be reimagined, realigned, rethought. The idea is one of an intellectual-imaginative process that is more metamorphic than metaphoric, in which there is no longer the illusion of 'any proper sense or figurative sense, only a distribution of states that is part of the range of the word'.[28] In this desire to de- and re-codify, Deleuze and Guattari appear to align philosophy closely with literature, just as Paterson aligns literature, and specifically poetry, with philosophy. 'We are born into a condition of metaphor', Paterson has claimed, detailing what he considers to be one of underpinning features of the human dream: 'a metaphor really being a contextual restriction of sense. We are attuned only to a small part of the electro-magnetic spectrum, and the universe our senses conjure up for us is not the universe'.[29] In this fashion, the poetic-philosophical project to which Paterson's verse appears to be increasingly directed is a process of deterritorialisation – interrogating routine encounters with the world, through the revivifying pressure of poetic language, so as the complex nature of wider reality begins to reveal itself. Rather than aspiring to the traditional poetic concept of metaphor in which one thing is shown to be similar to another, 'The White Lie' proposes a poetry that aspires to the metamorphosis of things actually taking from, feeding into, and 'becoming' one another, in the absence of any reified meanings. 'The point is never to leave the in-between', writes Niall Lucy of Deleuze and Guattari's philosophy, 'affirming the importance of coming and going rather than starting and finishing'.[30] The summary could as well serve as a pithy description of Paterson's *ars poetica*, and his imaginative, demanding, perceptually transformative poems.

Where 'The White Lie' departs from the anarchic propositions of Deleuze and Guattari's deterritorialisations is in its closing musings. These seem to return us to 'The Ferryman's Arms', and its hesitant recognition that any process of perceptual realignment – an apprehension of the human dream world through which we blunder – remains a necessarily partial one. In 'The White Lie', this is articulated with much greater verve and conviction, insisting that 'no one at one with all the universe / can touch one thing' (*SP* 115). Despite the powerful knowledge with which poetic thought's exposure of the human dream can supply us, 'we must', the poem argues, 'stay partly lost to find each other'. But if this is the case, as the narrator rightly questions, what 'earthly use are we' in saving one another? Occupying the 'supreme divorce' in which one isolated consciousness must necessarily remain from another, it is difficult to see how, as O'Brien puts it, we can use 'consciousness to redeem us from, well, consciousness'.[31] In the final quatrains of 'The White Lie', Paterson proposes that the possible solution to this dilemma lies in paradox: the paradox of poetry itself. 'Only by this – this shrewd obliquity / of speech, the broken word and the white lie, / do we check ourselves', the poem theorises (*SP* 115). Referring to 'this' very instance of poetic discourse, merging the twin deixis of 'this' moment of poetic composition and realisation with 'this' moment in which you, the reader, encounter the poet's words on the page, the poem announces its final thesis in the kind of self-aware, reflexive, direct register that defines so many of *Landing Light*'s poems. It is through poetry, that uniquely analytic means of tangentially approaching and imaginatively re-encountering ourselves and the world, that we can manage to more fully inhabit the divided state of mind necessary for responsible and meaningful understanding and action. This allows everything to be 'reconsumed in its estranging fire', while also retaining an anchoring sense of scale and order, 'that everything might keep the blackedged look / of things' (*SP* 116).

In the development of his oeuvre, *Landing Light* might be summarised as a volume that finds Paterson advancing his sense of poetry as a mode of knowledge in two ways. Its poems seek to define the problematic nature of human consciousness in the concept of 'the human dream', but they also reflexively assess and consciously enact poetry's capacity to successfully negotiate the riven state of being human. It is in Rainer Maria Rilke's vision of the lyric god Orpheus that Paterson attempts to find 'the ideal resolution to this potentially intolerable schism' (*O* 69).

5

Breath, You Invisible Poem: *Orpheus* (2006)

The philosophical treatise of *Landing Light*'s 'The White Lie' is in many ways the culmination of what Paterson has called 'his long and at times painful conversion to scientific materialism' (*O* 65). Yet this conversion is never quite complete for a poet who continues to value the imaginative intellectual potential of the broadly spiritual, alongside the rational rigours of scientific thought. 'Accomplishing this gave me some satisfaction', admits Paterson, 'but it left the room terribly quiet. I then sought some text I might get in my head as a *vade mecum*, whereby I could simply remember what I now held to be most true' (*O* 65). In this spirit, Paterson's fifth volume, a comprehensive translated 'version' of *The Sonnets to Orpheus* from the German of Rainer Maria Rilke, is something like a personal, secular holy book. 'In Rilke, as in Machado', Sean O'Brien has suggested, 'Paterson is drawn to a poet for whom ... poetry is an inimitable mode of knowledge'.[1] Just as Paterson found in Machado a poet thinking on matters both aesthetic and philosophical – poetry as anonymous and pure lyric utterance; faith as grounded conviction in the world's natural wonder – in Rilke, he sees a not dissimilar lyric ally. 'I was rather dismayed to discover the Sonnets' recent recruitment to the cause of "spiritual literature"', writes Paterson in the 'Afterword' to *Orpheus*:

> These days, this tends to denote a genre with no practical application beyond the invocation of a sort of difficult and torpid sense of well-being. Despite their continual invocation of the Singing God, and the vague pantheism Rilke occasionally conjures as symbolic of the connection we have lost to the Earth, the Sonnets are a

strongly non-religious work, and easily capable of an anti-religious interpretation. Though Rilke's myth – all half-light and demiurge – smacks of Gnosticism, he was not religious, and strove to locate all his spiritual wonder in the life we lead now. (O 66)

Again, Paterson is found delineating between religion and spirituality, restrictive dogma and imaginative wonder. For Paterson, Rilke is not the intense, distant, idiosyncratic, and often impenetrable poetic voice that English language readers have previously found him to be in translation. His own version of *The Sonnets to Orpheus* – fifty-five poems composed by Rilke in two weeks, that the German poet himself described as the 'dictation' of an 'inner impulse', and 'no intended or expected work'[2] – emerges from a desire to restore to the poems their rewarding modern complexity. But the version also succeeds in its lucidity and human warmth, that blend of thought and feeling in verse that Paterson has increasingly been drawn to since *The Eyes*. It is what Mark Doty has described, in a review of Paterson's *Orpheus*, as 'a true sense of an inhabited skin, a pulsing body responding to the life of the senses'.[3] These sonnets are also a crucial project in Paterson's stylistic development, given their specifically formal nature. As Hugh Haughton suggests, in an essay addressing what he dubs the 'Patersonnet', the sonnet form in Paterson's *Orpheus* 'produces a strong sense of renewal, in which Paterson develops his own speculative ontology'.[4] As in *The Eyes*, Paterson's intention in *Orpheus* is one of poetic reimagination. This takes the form of a dialogue between the spirit of the original and the imperative of lyric unity, which is to say the infusion of sound and sense that, for Paterson, is at the heart of the creation of any lyric poem, perhaps especially the sonnet. As Robert Vilain states: 'If Paterson's poems are versions they are therefore also replacements – not only in the sense of substitutes, but almost literally "re-placements."'[5]

The stylistic hallmark of *Orpheus* lies in its attempt to fully uncover the poetic utility of the sonnet. More than mere exercise, Paterson versions Rilke as a means of evincing his sense of the form as an inevitable necessity. While *Orpheus* announces Paterson's first extended engagement with the sonnet, we have already seen how the form establishes itself as a persistent fascination from the beginnings of his poetry. 'Nobody can say for certain where or when the sonnet originated', Paterson has argued in an extended essay on the form, 'but if some thirteenth-century Italian hadn't "invented" the sonnet, someone else would have: we would have arrived at the sonnet as we arrived at the wheel, out of evolutionary necessity'.[6] For a form that can typically seem quite markedly artificial, this is a bold and not uncontroversial claim to make, but it is one that Paterson expounds upon with considerable argumentative rigour. In many ways, it should not surprise that the sonnet has such powerful appeal for a poet who holds musical memorability and semantic cohesion as two of the most important features of the successful poem. His contention with regard to the sonnet's inevitability, and its success, is that the 'visual appeal of an approximately square field of black text on a sheet of white paper' must have been 'impossible to resist' as poetry moved from the oral tradition of folklore to the printed page.[7] 'Which is what the sonnet is, first and foremost', Paterson states, 'a small square poem' – one that, through virtue of its attempts to embody unity of meaning in a medium that can often resist such unity, also makes it a 'paradox, a little squared circle'.[8]

The underlying spiritual connotations of Paterson's concept of the sonnet as 'squared circle' are worth dwelling on. The specific notion and ancient puzzle of squaring the circle has long since proven to be an impossible geometrical task, but as a more broadly imaginative and symbolic idea, it has continuing ramifications. These are manifest in our human attempt to map the transcendent (with the symbol of the circle traditionally representing infinity and the divine) through the manmade (wherein the square represents structure and mechanical order), in the hope of bringing the natural world and the human world into realignment. The concept is referenced in much world literature: a pertinent example is in Dante's *Paradiso*, where an attempt to combine the divine and the human finds the poet struggling with an act that, the poem suggests, may be beyond human comprehension: 'As the geometer his mind applies / To square the circle, nor for all his wit / Finds the right formula, howe'er he tries, / So strove I with that wonder'.[9] On the evidence of his critical writings and many of the versioned sonnets after Rilke in *Orpheus*, Paterson's ambition appears to be a similar one, striving to somehow locate that 'spiritual wonder', as he puts it, 'in the life we lead now' (*O* 66).

Taking Rilke's lead, Paterson's 'Breath', his version of the first sonnet in Part Two of the Sonnets, is a manifestly elemental poem. It begins by addressing breath itself, the life force that makes speech and song possible, but that which is also being's 'counterbalance', a phenomenon that can equally take life away (*SP* 127). The natural rhythm and occurrence of breath makes it an apt subject to reflect Paterson's belief in the sonnet form's organic development. Breath is described as an 'invisible poem' no less, and one that is – uniquely to Paterson's reimagining – 'sister to silence'. The significance of the specific addition of this image emerges when considered alongside one of the 'Fourteen Notes on the Version', included in the appendix to *Orpheus*:

> Charles Simic once memorably said that poems are translations from the silence. For a version to be any kind of real poem, it must first reinhabit that extralinguistic silence the original poem once itself enjoyed – which is to say the poem must make a symbolic exit from language altogether. In this meditative space, its pattern of idea and image is reconsumed by its own strangeness, and when it re-emerges into language rediscovers itself in original speech. (*O* 75)

On one level, Paterson is here proposing that all 'real' poems – whether they be versions or more purely original compositions – can only come into existence if the poet is able to access 'that extralinguistic silence', which is to say the mysteriously subconscious realm from which he believes the true poem tends to emerge, explored in poems such as 'The Rat' and 'A Fraud' in *Landing Light*. But on another level, just as the poem is able to combine mystery with sense through this simultaneously conscious and unconscious process, he is also suggesting that poems are especially well placed to combine the spiritual with the rational, to make a monistic whole of world and human. 'What estates, // what vast spaces have already poured through my lungs?' asks the poet: 'The four winds / are like daughters to me' (*SP* 127). The suggestion is that even the simple act of breathing can deliver a striking new knowledge of the interrelation of our human selves and the wider world, if due attention and poetic reimagination are brought to bear upon it. And so, suddenly, the 'slow wave' of breath is the 'ocean I accumulate

/ by stealth', an unbroken connection between our breathing selves and the whole troposphere. As Stephen Mitchell notes in the foreword to his translations of Rilke: 'By the end of The Sonnets, Rilke is no longer addressing Orpheus, the primal poet. He has become Orpheus and can speak to his personal self from the centre of the universe. The cycle is completed. Life resolves in a single breath.'[10] Certainly, 'Breath' looks to briefly square the circle in its metaphorical doubling: breath is a passport to commune with the universe, and it is also a guarantor of the poem, of language, and the individual's subjective apprehensions. But in a fashion as much Patersonian as Rilkean, the moment of pure transcendence, the promise of the isolated human consciousness achieving oneness with the matter of the universe, is still inevitably, necessarily, indefinitely deferred. 'So do you know me, air, that once sailed through me?' enquires the poet (*SP* 127). The air might once have been 'the leaf and rind' of every word the poet has spoken, but there is always a disconnection between the thinking matter of our being and the incomprehensible indifference of invisible forces, swirling across the globe.

Paterson's version of the fifth sonnet of Part Two, 'Anemone', can be read as an attempt to map this disconnection. The poem reads as an extended metaphor, exploring the human fear that stems from our self-preserving inability to fully transcend the perceptual limitations of the human dream. The eponymous flower of the poem begins by 'creaking open to the dawn', nourished by photosynthesis. But it is not long before the sun's intensity 'floods her white lap till she drowns', given the 'tiny muscle' at the personified flower's centre, which is, we are told, 'tensed to open to the All' (*SP* 128). Paterson's version agrees with Rilke's original insofar as it suggests that the anemone's is a pure receptivity, one that humankind has become largely incapable of despite our superior ability to thrive and survive. 'In our violence, we outlive her', Paterson claims. 'But which new life will see us flower / and face the skies, as true receivers?'

What Paterson's poem rearticulates through Rilke is exactly this recognition – of the delimiting price of our cynical and manipulative human exploits, and consequent detachment from the universe. We might 'outlive' the anemone, but at what cost? The implication is that a shorter life of truer and more meaningful connection with the natural world may in fact be preferable, especially since our 'violence' will prove ultimately destructive to ourselves, and not to the indifference of an eternal universe of which we are a fleeting part. It is this human fear that Paterson's poem knowingly projects onto the anemone when the speaker claims 'she barely heeds the sunset's call // or finds the willpower to refurl / her petal-edges'. We cannot understand the seeming abandon of the anemone, the poem suggests, which is 'open to the All' in spite of the risks such openness involves. But as a poem that refashions a Rilke original, 'Anemone' can also be read as Paterson paying homage to Rilke's own sensibility and artistic resolve. As the German poet wrote in a letter at about the time of the Sonnets' composition: 'I am like the anemone I once saw in a garden in Rome ... in the dark meadow, wide open, still taking everything in ... and alongside, all its prudent sisters, each one closed.'[11] In its correlation with his sense of the poet as one engaged in the dangerous business of interrogating their own unconscious and sensory perceptions, Paterson clearly admires this personal characteristic, and the way it announces itself in Rilke's Sonnets. Through Paterson's understanding of Rilke, the sonnet form emerges as 'a box for the poet's dreams'[12] that, like the anemone, is capable of closing around 'its small measure of profusion', but also of 'opening to the All' (*SP* 128). Rilke's sonneteering even leads Paterson to suggest that it sets the poet apart as a prophet of sorts:

> In an earlier age we would have had no trouble in describing the Sonnets – in the manner of their composition, their lucid vision of the future, their oracular turn of phrase – as a prophetic book. Which would make Rilke a prophet of sorts; perhaps a fair description, if what you mean by prophet is someone so sensitive that they become not only a lightning rod for all the crackling static of the culture, but also a satellite-dish, a 'receiver' (to use a Rilkean favourite) for things a less precisely attuned and calibrated sensibility would never be aware of. These individuals possess no supernatural powers, but do have an abnormally strong sense of what's on the wind for us. (*O* 62–3)

Orpheus as a collection is perhaps best understood as Paterson's personal, secular holy book. Extending his unique take on the *via negativa*, first outlined in *God's Gift to Women*'s 'Prologue' and *The Eyes*' 'Profession of Faith' (alongside the distinction these poems draw between the restrictions of religious dogma and the possibilities of spiritual wonder), the versioning of Rilke's Sonnets clearly offered Paterson a means of further scrutinising the nature of the human dream, and the existential conundrum of being human. 'The two principle religious errors seem to me beautifully refuted in the Sonnets', Paterson writes in the 'Afterword' to the volume. 'The first is to think of truth as being in possession of an inscrutable third party, whose knowledge and intentions can only be divined' (*O* 66). This reallocation of meaning-making and agency from unspecified deity to ourselves – a stance warranted by the fact that, as Paterson argues, 'we are all the thinking that matter is doing in this part of the universe' – is one that we have already seen broached elsewhere. The notion that any truly meaningful sense of reality effectively resides in the eye of the beholder, a world-making imaginative power that can serve as both blessing and curse, is further explored in a number of Paterson's *Orpheus* poems.

This ties in with the second 'religious error' that Paterson argues the Sonnets neatly refute. This is essentially the idea that whatever afterlife we are apparently bound for is *the* truly miraculous state, while our current life on Earth is demoted to the mere status of 'existential preamble' (*O* 67). Paterson's argument is that much organised religion is responsible for further cementing the human dream in this way. If we are encouraged to fully project ourselves into a future beyond our deaths, this can only serve to damage our sense of responsibility to the here and now. 'Religion acts as if it holds the copyright on the miraculous', Paterson chides, 'and yet it is dedicated to eradicating the *real* wonder from the human experience' (*O* 67–68).

This 'real wonder', in Paterson's take on the Sonnets, is what it is to be *here*, making sense of the everyday mystery of the world through pushing our cerebral faculties to the limits of their emotional and intellectual understanding. If there is a medium through which such efforts can be fully focused and maximised, for Paterson it is poetry. Criticising the manner in which poems have been increasingly viewed, since Modernism's heyday in the 1920s, as completely unparaphrasable works that must be painstakingly interpreted in and of themselves, he suggests that the poem is unfortunately 'now rarely treated as a direct and trustworthy form of human discourse' (O 64). For Paterson, however, 'the Sonnets, for all their occasional obscurity, make a great deal of plain sense', and it is this sense that he wants to see 'placed at heart of any discussion if the poems are actually to be *useful* to us, and perhaps at the heart of all discussion of poetry if we are to both legitimise and encourage its original thinking as well as its original speech' (O 65). Poetry as a fully fledged mode of knowledge, no less.

'The Double Realm', Paterson's version of Rilke's sonnet VI from Part One of the *Sonette*, is a poem that finds Orpheus as the 'true emblem' of this imaginative endeavour (O 8). Discussing what he views as the 'informing insight of the Sonnets', Paterson outlines that 'Man is probably unique amongst the mammals in that he has conscious foreknowledge of his death' (O 68). As such, 'knowing he will die means he acts, in part, as if he were already dead'. In Rilke's Sonnets, the mythic Orpheus, descending to the Underworld only to return to the land of the living, is the 'man who has found the perfect balance between death and life, eternity and the living present': what Paterson summarises as 'the ideal possessor of the "double realm"' (O 69). It is this transgressive condition of ghosthood that Paterson suggests might 'inform our behaviour' in both positive and negative ways – it is our human choice, in other words, in the meaning we make of the world through our imaginative faculties, and in choosing to explore the mysteries of that tangible world and our part in it. 'Does he belong here?' the speaker asks us of Orpheus in 'The Double Realm': 'No, his spacious nature / had its birth in both realms' (O 8). Orpheus is, like all of us, a person divided, but as the lyric god, he is also especially capable of bridging that divide, an example to the rest of us. As the poem suggests: 'But he can *raise* the dead, / and conjured through his half-transparent lids / confuses that dark land in everything'. As such, the sudden magical properties of 'earth-smoke' and 'meadow-rue' appear to Orpheus 'as real as their bright bloom' – the human dream is both recognised and briefly transcended, so that the human sense, but also the wider mystery, of each object is revealed. As Paterson speculates in an aphorism from *The Book of Shadows*: 'If the object is allowed to shrug off its name, it begins the long road back to its own intrinsic mystery' (*TBS* 13).

In this way, the poem proposes that we might partly emulate the lyric god, despite lacking his supernatural powers, and so more widely understand ourselves and the world around us. To quote Antonio Porchia, outlined in previous chapters as a significant influence on Paterson's poetic thinking: 'The shadows: some hide, others reveal'; elsewhere, Porchia has gnomically claimed that 'sometimes at night, I light a lamp so as not to see'.[13] As we have seen throughout Paterson's oeuvre, the darkness can often harbour strangely illuminating truths – certainly as many as the cold light of day. Through Rilke's example, 'The Double Realm' suggests Orpheus as the exemplar of this discerning awareness: 'whether lifted from the hearth or the cold clay', he is apparently capable of reimagining, and so reigniting the possibility within, 'pitcher, torque and ring' (*O* 8). This Orphic, stereoscopic view of life is one that is even more emphatically championed elsewhere in *Orpheus*.

'The thirteenth sonnet of the second part is for me the most valid of all', Rilke proclaimed in a letter to Katharina Kippenberg: 'It includes all the others, and it expresses that which – though it still far exceeds me – my purest, most final achievement would someday, in the midst of life, have to be.'[14] Rilke died shortly after the composition and publication of the *Sonette*, and on Paterson's reading and versioning of this especially significant sonnet in *Orpheus*, the controversial suggestion is that this should, in some ways, come as no surprise. Extending his belief in Rilke's prophetic sensibility and attunement, Paterson argues that the German poet 'was flying his kite in a thunderstorm':

> Certain kinds of art practice are constitutionally dangerous. We are real objects in the universe, and so just as affected by vibration as anything else; however, we continually act as if we're immune, and tend to dismiss the 'sufferings of the artist' as either mere drama-queenery or, at best, neurotic excess. They can be both those things, certainly; but artists also put themselves in the way of a dangerous kind of sympathetic resonance. Who knows what remote and inhuman harmony Rilke inadvertently conducted in their composition; but my hunch is that, even mediated, tamed and humanised by his great formal mastery, it probably still killed him,

even if the effects were delayed: the mind is part of the body, and they share one another's ills. (*O* 63)

We have already seen how Paterson's poems and critical writings demonstrate a sense of the mortal perils of composing an authentic poetry, one that is committed to the active, interrogative pursuit of renewed understanding. For Paterson, the close scrutiny of one's own unconscious, combined with the jolting perceptual realignment that even a brief escape from the comforts of the human dream can provide, puts the poet 'in the way of a dangerous kind of sympathetic resonance'. In Rilke, he appears to find an example of this taken to its extreme, unguarded, almost foolhardy conclusion – and nowhere is Rilke's personal fate more apparent than in the argument put forward by sonnet XIII from Part Two. It certainly seems prescient of Rilke to have identified the poem as his 'final achievement' – in the sense that it is a major poem within the sequence, but more so in the grave sense of being a poetic last will and testament.

Paterson's version is titled 'The Passing', a reference both to the intensely felt yet paradoxically passive resolve that Rilke's original advocates as a state of being, but also to the German poet's impending mortal demise. 'Be ahead of all departure', Paterson writes, 'learn to act / as if, like the last winter, it was all over' (*SP* 130). Comparing the opening quatrain of Paterson's version to that of Stephen Mitchell's translation of Rilke's original points up some telling distinctions. Rather than opting for the more nuanced meaning of 'the last winter' as Paterson does, announcing an aptly grave finality, Mitchell renders Rilke's lines as simply referring to 'the winter that has just gone by'.[15] Moreover, while Mitchell and Paterson talk similarly of the 'exact' winter that Rilke's poem suggests must be withstood, Mitchell renders Rilke as proposing that this will ensure the heart simply 'survives', whereas Paterson's version finds the poet announcing that 'your heart will last for ever'. The pertinence of these differences is best understood in the distinction between the act of translation and the act of imaginative versioning. 'This is not a translation, but a version', writes Paterson in 'Fourteen Notes on the Version', a short essay in the appendix to *Orpheus*: 'A translation tries to remain true to the original words and their relations ... It glosses the original, but does not try to replace it.

Versions, however, are trying to be poems in their own right'
(*O* 73). While we might variously disagree over the degree to
which translations harbour an always exacting felicity to the
original, and to which versions succeed as fully fledged poems,
this statement is nevertheless useful in understanding Paterson's
significant departure from Rilke's original in the case of 'The
Passing'. Whereas Mitchell's translation project is framed by its
attempt to smoothly transpose Rilke from German to English
as the inferred poet-speaker of the Sonnets, Paterson's *Orpheus*
announces its distinctive multiplicity of address, one that finds
its origins in his especially complex understanding of direct
address and poem–reader relations, illustrated in discussion of
Landing Light in the previous chapter.

From the volume's title – *Orpheus* – we therefore infer that
these are poems spoken with a timeless and anonymous lyric
voice, sonnets as much 'to' Orpheus as they are 'to' Rilke and
to the anticipated variety of listeners they might encounter,
as well as poems that occasionally speak on behalf of Rilke.
They are poems that look forward but that also listen back,
inhabiting the 'double realm' through keeping one eye on the
living present – their immediacy of address; their modern
adaptation of Rilke's ever-relevant thematic concerns – and
one eye on the past: not least the strange circumstances of the
original sonnets' composition. In this manner, Paterson's version
of 'The Passing' is both a reflection of Rilke's philosophy, but
also a sceptical commentary on the extremes to which Rilke's
sacrifice to lyric drive and inspiration would lead. As such,
'The Passing' amplifies the tone of the original, giving the clear
sense of a voice in the grip of prophetic – but also potentially
self-annihilating – enlightenment. The dubious immortality that
Paterson has the poem's speaker promise us – 'your heart will
last for ever', but also the instruction to 'die', 'that you might
pass / into the pure accord' – is one example of this (*SP* 130).
Another is the imperative to 'be the glass / that shatters in the
sound of its own ringing'. In the 'Afterword' to *Orpheus*, it is
telling that Paterson confesses to having considered rendering
Rilke's original phrase of *zerschlug* – meaning something like
'shattered' or 'smashed' – as 'shiver' or 'tremble', on account that
'a shattered glass is no use to anyone' (*O* 63). There is obvious
concern on Paterson's part in regard to the Rilkean willingness

to 'unwisely' put oneself in the way of too much 'sympathetic resonance'.

In the event, 'The Passing' emerges as a poem that approves of Rilke's philosophy, but with an important reservation. Paterson espouses Rilke's view that we should sing with the 'sound of our own ringing' (*SP* 130); like the poetic-philosophical treatise outlined in *Landing Light*'s 'The White Lie', this invokes an imaginative detachment from the restrictions of sense that the human dream imposes, allowing for a partial reconnection with our elemental, earthly home. Yet much as 'The White Lie' outlines the importance of poetry as perceptual reawakening with a concomitant commitment to the structure of sense and order – 'the poets' beautiful tightrope-walk ... the one between sense and mystery'[16] – it is Rilke's apprehension of Orpheus's dual view of life and death, a more balanced perspective, of which Paterson approves. Where Rilke veers towards the potentially self-destructive abandon proposed in certain Sonnets, Paterson is less convinced. 'Take all of nature, its one vast aggregate', 'The Passing' advises in its final lines, 'jubilantly multiply it by / the nothing of yourself, and clear the slate'. On the one hand, through the example of Rilke's bold assertions, Paterson is further advocating the loss of self – which is to say that of the narrowly human – to the monistic world at large. But on the other, the finality of the phrase 'clear the slate' infers the danger of embracing a full departure from our evolutionarily conditioned means of engaging with the world, and with one another. The complete erasure offered by the death realm, an Orphic Underworld that is 'fully honoured', is simply pure annihilation, which Paterson suggests is 'no use to anyone'.

In discussion of the sonnet 'Poetry' – the manifesto-in-miniature at the heart of *The Eyes* – we found Paterson first fully aligning himself with the aesthetics of poetic anonymity. The exploratory play with personae in *God's Gift to Women*, moving beyond T. S. Eliot's conscious workshopping of the self towards a poetry that inevitably undoes the self, saw Paterson's poetry establish a new emotional urgency and seriousness for itself through adopting Machado's example. 'Poetry' suggests that the communal medium of language itself, in which the initial feeling that ignites the poem is tempered and universalised, should be the primary agent in poetic discourse, allowing for poems that both speak of and manage to invoke shared emotion, underpinned by sharp critical thinking. The result, when successful, is a poetry that combines felt immediacy – the powerful illusion of the present moment, and a present speaker – with timeless poetic intelligence and wisdom. Increasingly, this appears to be the ambitious aim of Paterson's verse, what Sean O'Brien describes as 'a shedding of particulars in pursuit of a final adaptability'.[17] It is an attempt, in other words, to extract the resonant moment of existential revelation and perceptual clarity from the otherwise irrelevant aspects of circumstance and modernity that surround it.

In *Orpheus*, Paterson uncovers Rilke as a poetic ally in his sense of verse's transcendental potential. 'Ultimately there is only one poet', Rilke wrote in 1920, 'that infinite one who makes himself felt, here and there through the ages, in a mind that can surrender to him'.[18] For Rilke, it is clearly the case that the 'one poet' is Orpheus, the lyric god who, through the captivating medium of song, charms all creatures through the musical truth of his lyre – a musical truth, and way of being, that Rilke sought to emulate in his *Sonette*. As Paterson's 'Leaving' puts it, echoing Rilke's original lines: '*Orpheus*, we say / wherever the true song is manifest' (*SP* 119). But for Paterson, the troublesome issue remains in the fate that met with Rilke, in seeming to surrender himself to – and so confuse himself with – the lyric god. 'Rilke knew he was singing more clearly than he ever had', as the 'Afterword' states, 'and – feeling himself so strongly in the god's grip, *one appointed to praise* – at times conflates himself with the singing god almost unthinkingly. This is self-astonishment as much as it is arrogance, and we forgive this as easily as we forgive Dante his vanities in the *Commedia*' (*O* 61). What Paterson is primarily looking for in Rilke, and in the figure of Orpheus, is a means of inhabiting something of what he sees as the 'true song', but one with a more level-headed, recognisably human message.

'A God', Paterson's version after sonnet III of Part One of the *Sonette*, is a poem about the difficulty of imitating a deity like Orpheus. But it also departs from Rilke's original, in clearly addressing the dangers of such imitation. What the poet might learn from Orpheus's example is one thing; the damage of confusing oneself with the lyric god is quite another. 'A god can do it. But will you tell me how / a man can enter through the lyre's strings?' implores the poet-speaker in Stephen Mitchell's broadly faithful translation of Rilke's original.[19] In Paterson's 'A God', the question is put rather differently: 'But how can a man follow, / will someone tell me, through the narrow lyre?' (O 5). This sounds a note of incredulity at Rilke's endeavour, but also suggests a historical awareness of the fate that, in Paterson's view, met with Rilke as a result of the Sonnets' 'dictation'. Similarly, the answer in 'A God' is much more definite than the original: 'His mind is cloven. No temple to Apollo / can rise at such a crossroads' (O 5). Man and god are simply different creatures, with different capabilities.

In spite of the pronounced scepticism in the poem's opening lines, rejecting the plain imitation of Orpheus, the remainder of 'A God' serves to outline what the mortal poet can learn from the lyric god, acting as an extension of the *ars poetica* first outlined in 'Poetry' from *The Eyes*. 'Song is not desire; so you taught', the speaker announces: 'Nor is it courtship, nor is it courtship's prize. / Song is being' (O 5). We have returned, in part, to the Machadian territory of the 'bright coal' of the poet's love as it 'begins to smoulder', smothering the deeply reflective anonymity of the 'pure verse' in an excess of personal, 'boastful' feeling (*SP* 71). But what Paterson also uncovers in 'A God', through Rilke's commune with Orpheus, is a clearer distinction between the 'kinds of breath' that are the life force of 'true singing', which is to say the true poem, balanced between sound and silence. 'Youth – / don't fool yourself that love unlocks this art', the poet-speaker reprimands the would-be poet in the sonnet's decisive turn, as if suddenly channelling the voice of Orpheus himself (O 5). The suggestion is that, while the poet might conjure verse from 'the sudden songs' that come with 'love's voice', these are inauthentic and fleeting: 'They'll end'. 'True singing is another kind of breath', the poem quietly concludes of lasting verse: 'A breath of nothing. A sigh in a god. A wind.'

The purpose to which Paterson's individual take on the *via negativa* has long been directed appears to reach its pinnacle in the terseness of this Rilkean revelation. As was first mooted in the concluding lines of 'A Private Bottling' in *God's Gift to Women*, where the speaker admonishes himself to keep the 'sentimental residue' of experience sharply in view while raising the 'purely / offertory glass that tastes of nothing / but silence', for Paterson, as for Rilke, it is in contemplation of absence, of the sound and sensation of nothing itself, where poetic clarity and truth resides (*SP* 36). It is here, Paterson suggests, that our perceptions are able to briefly escape the blinkered concerns of the individual self. *Song* – the combination of lyric and music that is 'unique' to humankind, offering 'a stay against time's passing'[20] – *is being*: an awareness of the self, and its mortality, in the here-and-now of the universe and time's flow towards nothingness, to entropy's absolute absence. *Gesang ist Dasein*: in so versioning Rilke's phrase, Paterson creates a concise aphorism for that which has preoccupied his poetry from the outset – the nature of existence and human consciousness, understood in both broadly spiritual and scientific-materialist terms; and how to develop an ontology to make fuller sense of that very existential dilemma through the medium of poetry. The answer, it appears, is in the singing line that conflates sound and sense, allowing for the extralinguistic perceptual transformation that can conjure a presence out of absence, finding sustaining meaning where, outside of our human perception, there is none. As Paterson argues in *The Poem*: 'For its ability to unite our choppy and fragmented perception by singing across the gaps, song has long been our aspirational archetype … Orpheus used song to cross the ultimate dividing border, and defy death itself.'[21] But such 'songs' as lyric poems must be precisely calibrated and carefully weighted, if they are to utilise language to reach for emotion and understanding beyond language itself. 'He who tells the truth says almost nothing', Antonio Porchia once claimed, while also suggesting that 'only a few arrive at nothing, because the way is long'.[22] It is the pared-back clarity and minimalist diction of the most successful poems in Paterson's sixth volume, *Rain*, that illustrate these maxims in action. Here the very act of poetry becomes an enterprise and art form to be continually suspected, queried, and stripped back.

6

None of This Matters: *Rain* (2009)

In his collection of aphorisms *The Book of Shadows*, Paterson outlines the 'four lives' of the poet – or rather, the stages through which he suggests the lyric poet passes in their increasing understanding of the art. Having first shed their 'lyric innocence', we are told that they then awaken to the fact that a poet is *someone whom words continually fail'* (*TBS* 83). *Landing Light* showed Paterson entering the third stage of this chronology: by now thoroughly suspicious of his art, the poet decides to 'leave the tiny house of the poem to inspect the façade, and learn something of the architectural mysteries he once had no desire to penetrate'. Piercing enquiries into the nature of poetic composition and the self, alongside the interrogative assessment of poetry's imaginative capacities as a unique means of exploring the human condition, are characteristic of *Landing Light* as a whole. In its varying forms, tonal shifts, and artistic scope, the collection undoubtedly stands as Paterson's most wide-ranging. Yet rather than an intensification of this expansiveness, the 'fourth stage' that Paterson identifies in the poet's life suggests a return, perhaps wishfully, to the innocence of that original 'lyric muse' – an innocence that Paterson suggests must be 'conscientiously, even cynically defended' (*TBS* 83).

Whether or not this seriocomic aphorism rings true is one thing; what it might imply as a personal reflection on the unusual trajectory of Paterson's career is another. *Rain*, Paterson's sixth volume, can be viewed as a book that reveals his poetry entering into this 'phase' of lyrical clarity. The experienced poet can never hope to unthink the knowledge that a long apprenticeship in the art of poetry brings, but where a poet as able as Paterson is concerned, said knowledge can have a curious effect on the style of their writing. After all, the marked stylistic shifts between Paterson's collections, alongside his unusual understanding and application of poetry as a unique mode of knowledge, are what mark him out among his contemporaries. In her review of *Rain*, A. E. Stallings suggests that we might expect an 'easy breeziness, a breathiness' in a poet's later work. Instead, as she observes, 'Paterson's poems have become more grounded ... and have a noon-day clarity with sharp shadows.'[1]

'Only the rarest artists move towards simplicity'. So Paterson has claimed, stating that 'the rest progress, which invariably means complication, as if you measured your advance by the number of readers you leave behind' (*TBS* 42). While not explicitly inferring his own work in this statement, Paterson is nevertheless outlining a particular, and doubtless personal, artistic ambition – one that he has set about attempting to fulfil. In his *ars poetica*, this notion is given a broader critical footing, in a tripartite outline of what Paterson views to be poetry's 'most powerful mnemonic devices': brief speech, patterned speech, and original speech. 'Brevity of speech is the poem's most basic formal strategy; originality of speech, its most basic literary virtue; patterned speech, its most basic identifying feature', he argues, before going on to suggest that 'the mere act of making brief speech often produces both original and patterned speech'.[2]

It is this call for clarity and brevity that finds its apogee in the poems of *Rain*. Given Paterson's acute awareness of poetry's shortcomings – how the poem's inventive utilisation of the flawed medium of language can often serve, in the end, only to outline how 'the word, in fact, falls terribly short of the world' (*TBS* 83) – combined with his bold ambition to realise poetry as a means of intellectual enquiry, the shift in style seems to announce a natural progression. 'Only the best poets can risk simplicity', Paterson reiterates in an aphorism from *The Blind Eye*: 'The rest of us are merely exposed by it. Only those same poets can risk complexity too: the rest invariably fail to realise the greatly increased responsibility towards clarity that it demands' (*BE* 27). Brevity and clarity, in other words, are in Paterson's view essential components of a poetic aesthetic that seeks not only to uncover the myriad complexities of the human condition and the universe we find ourselves situated within, but to also make useful sense of them, equipping both poet and reader with the ability to reconceptualise, reimagine and so, on some level, remake the world before them.

In charting the stylistic development of Paterson's oeuvre, we have uncovered poetic form (and the imaginative processes it can enable) as an abiding fascination. Paterson's frequent adherence to poetic forms – whether conventional, adapted, or self-invented – rarely find him paying mere lip service to some misguided notion of tradition. Rather, his sense and use of form is an active, purposeful, and energising one, what Michael Donaghy once called the 'serendipity provided by negotiation with a resistant medium'.[3] Briefly freeing the poet from conscious thought, it is this approach that enables the kind of intellectually and emotionally transformative effects that Paterson prizes so highly, in his commitment to the poem as a means of generating new understanding.

'The Lie', a haunting poem in *Rain* that describes an invented but strangely tangible creature called The Lie, at first invites a straightforward reading. Its sophisticated use of end-rhyme, employing only two rhymes throughout its five quatrains and final two lines, gives plainspoken voice to a narrator who is found confessing to a disturbing ritual. Each day, we are told, he rises 'before the house had woken' to attend to the 'drip' and secure the 'shackles' of The Lie, who, it transpires, is secretly locked up in his basement. Practised as he is in this 'chore', the speaker coolly states that he had 'counted maybe thirteen years or more / since last I'd felt the urge to meet his eye' (*SP* 146). However, during one such routine inspection, he accidentally catches the gag of The Lie, tearing it away. At this, The Lie is revealed to be 'a boy of maybe three or four', sickly and grim, who asks – in a tone that may suggest knowing accusation as much as apparent innocence – '*Why do you call me The Lie?*' Dumbfounded or else appalled, the narrator tells how he 'could make him no reply', before he hurriedly retied the gag 'as tight as it would tie' and 'locked the door and locked the door and locked the door'.

The poem's subject matter appears to be psychological repression. Given the fictional, figurative nature of 'The Lie', the obvious implication is that the narrator has something terrifying locked up in his psychic basement, the traumatic memory of a past experience that he cannot forget or rid himself, finding its symbolic and literal embodiment as a creature he must dutifully, and sometimes painfully, attend to. As Sean O'Brien has argued: 'Perhaps the force of this strange, powerful, terrible poem arises from the strategy of not revealing what the story behind the secret is: the imprisoned Lie can seem to speak to anyone.'[4] There is certainly a disturbing open-endedness to the poem's unusual use of metaphor: rather than the conventional processes by which we might expect a lyric poem to suggestively describe one thing in terms of another, inviting a renewed apprehension of both things, 'The Lie' seems more allegorical. Its symbolic figure of the eponymous Lie comes to represent whatever awful self-torment or unspeakable self-deception the reader's mind inevitably projects into it.

In this way, the poem can be seen to make use of, and support the case for, Paterson's argument that intelligible meaning 'just isn't in residence anywhere', whether that be in poems or in other instances of discourse.[5] Rather, as 'The Lie' serves to manipulate and illustrate, meaning is instead *generated*, produced by our active and intelligent engagement, and occurs in poems within 'the dynamic flux of our reading and rereading'.[6] In the absence of any clear outline of what The Lie might specifically represent, the poem invites the reader's thoughts to rush in and fill the void it has created. Whether real or imagined, we all have our version of The Lie, and 'The Lie' calculates for that very fact, manipulating our tendency to *read in* and seek out meaning. What the reader gets for their trouble, like the poet, is a stark awakening to whatever sinister personal torment might be concerning them, before the poem mercifully silences it, and attempts to lock up the mind's cellar.

Yet, as one critic has argued, it is likely 'too simple and clinical to say that this poem deals only with repression and the dawning of some horrified self-awareness'.[7] Paying attention to the poem's formal qualities as well as its inferred thematic content might equally suggest that 'The Lie' is a poem about 'the lie' of poetry itself. A Paterson poem is unusually and intelligently conscious of itself, and by extension all poetry, as a necessary fiction, a manmade work of inevitable artifice. But while many of Paterson's poems serve to sharply illustrate the ever-present gap between our everyday use of language and the complexities of the physical world beyond human perception, they are also demonstrably committed to serving a real-world purpose. This is most apparent in Paterson's sense of the art form as a means of imaginatively turning language against its original purpose of staid conceptual division, bridging the divide between our linguistically shaped encounters with the world, and the mysterious nature of reality beyond 'the human dream'. As Paterson has claimed in interview: 'Poetic language has two functions; to make things clear and distinct where they weren't, and to join them back up again when they were broken apart. It's a natural function of language, and the way that language, certainly, redeems itself.'[8]

It is this key tension – between poetry's promise as a genuine mode of knowledge, and the poet's inevitable resort to sleights of hand in what is, fundamentally, the poem's manufactured text-world – that appears to have driven so much of Paterson's composition over the years. In the process he has become, as one critic has noted, 'both pursuer and pursued', a poet of such a calibre that his fate is, perhaps, to be 'chased offstage by the art he once chased'.[9] In 'The Lie', there are numerous suggestions that propose that it is the very craft of poetry itself that is 'locked' in the psychic basement of the poet-speaker's mind. The 'shackles' that bind The Lie and that the narrator is at pains to keep secure despite the creature's obvious lack of resistance, find their equivalence in the steady iambic pentameter of the poem (*SP* 146). Though the situation is a strange one – both in the sense of the narrator's entrapment of The Lie, and in the peculiar act of the reader's engagement with the poem – everything is apparently under control, both literally and metrically. After all, the speaker is 'so practised' in the 'chore' of revivifying and otherwise attending to The Lie ('his drip changed'), that he has 'counted maybe thirteen years or more' since he last met 'his eye'.

In many ways, the 'rapport' between the two is like that of the accomplished poet's relationship with his craft: something they may be able to engage with so routinely that they fall into the habit of versifying in an altogether habitual, non-interrogative manner. The speaker's testing of the 'ligature' binding The Lie reinforces this interpretation, if we consider that, as well as defining the act of tying and binding in a literal sense, 'ligature'

99

also more figuratively refers to anything that unifies or bonds together – the lyric unity of the poem, no less. But if, as the poem suggests, this unity becomes mere rehearsal, and no more than a forced and habitual process such as that of the narrator's relationship with The Lie, it serves to be both emotionally inauthentic (refusing to look at oneself, and one's poetic practice, with clear-eyed perspicacity) and even abusive. At best, it is nothing more than a 'chore' – for the narrator checking on his Lie, morning after morning, and for author and reader alike. A poet might possess the two sides of the self that are necessary for true poetic composition: the manipulative conscious mind and the unbidden spontaneity of unrehearsed sensibility. But unless the poet remains vigilant and sufficiently demanding of their writing, their verse in time might simply turn into tired habit.

Remaining authentic to the vocation of poet is, for Paterson, to feel 'the urge to meet the eye' of whatever is locked deep in the unconscious, to entertain Rilke's example of the Orphic path, and to 'access those darker corridors of the memory and imagination from which we might recover the true poem'.[10] It is the poet-speaker's sudden reawakening to this fact, and the consequent fear that this instils, that determines his reaction to The Lie's question: *'Why do you call me The Lie?'* He cannot make a reply because it is a fair question and he knows it: The Lie may be a fiction in so far as he is the product of the poet-speaker's imagination, but he is an altogether real torment, as real as the poem to which he gives his name, and as real as its disturbing effects. As Paterson has long claimed, if we accept that the way we look at the world is all there is of the world (at least as we know it), then rather than being distinct from it, 'the imagination is how we correct reality for error'.

The Lie ends up being one such correction, a reminder of why the poet can sometimes 'hate the very poem that they are writing', as Dan Chiasson has claimed, 'in language brilliant and moving enough to convey how useless and phony the language of poetry is'.[11] The crafted, complexly end-rhymed quatrains of the poem, the deftly controlled metre and lyric poise, only serve in the end to undermine themselves and the poet-speaker, collapsing from crafted elegance and structured order into a frantic rush to 'lock the door' of the poem shut, before The Lie 'could say more' (*SP* 146). In this manner, 'The Lie' can be seen to suggest that the more capable, committed, imaginatively, and formally resourceful the poet, the more apparent to them the shortcomings of any form of poetic craft are. This leaves them chastened and uncertain, but also with a peculiarly advanced understanding of the art form's claims to authenticity, and its limitations.

Paterson has a keenly metaphysical interest in the dilemma of human consciousness. His work assesses the challenges that the human dream poses for a poetry whose purpose and ambition is to 'articulate new concepts that the language can't yet accommodate'.[12] As our discussion of 'The White Lie' revealed, 'only by this … shrewd obliquity / of speech' can we hope to 'check ourselves' (*SP* 115). Poetry is a unique means of weighing our evolutionarily conditioned means of engagement ('the blackedged / look of things') against the often inaccessible nature of a reality beyond such habitual perception, as the world is 'reconsumed in its estranging fire' through the transformative force of poetic language (*SP* 114).

In *Rain*, Paterson exploits this understanding, and his consequently ambitious sense of poetry's purpose to its fullest heights, in poems that make a virtue of both verse's knowledge-generating capabilities and its inevitable shortcomings. A poem such as 'The Lie' manages both to convincingly assert and undermine poetry's potential – in its form, its necessary artifice, its structures and fractures, and in its musically dependent meaning-making. As an accomplished jazz guitarist of many years, it is unsurprising that musicality and song – which are central to his appreciation of Rilke's adaptation of the Orpheus myth – should figure so strongly in Paterson's concept of the lyric poem. 'The lovely thing about music', he once stated in a radio interview, 'is that it is a pure medium – all you need is the air and some silence. Whereas poetry has a problem because its medium is language, so it's kind of a meta-art if you like, it has to ride on the structure of language for its meaning.'[13]

By these lights, music appears to be the superior art form, at which point one might ask why an able musician who believes this would choose to write poetry at all. But while Paterson argues the case for music as a more effective means of making immediate emotional sense, he clearly believes that poetry, however compromised it may be by language's intrinsic shortcomings, is the only cerebral means to bridge what he calls 'the epistemic asymmetry between the inner and outer realms',[14] which is to say the distorted perceptual divide between the isolated self and the wider world. In his *ars poetica* treatise *The Poem*, this process is outlined as one dependent on the concept of 'trope'. As Paterson suggests, the term 'trope' is commonly used to refer to 'a figurative or metaphorical expression', while in rhetoric it describes 'a word or phrase that "turns" from its normal use'.[15] Here the term is adapted to a specifically poetic purpose, however, to 'describe the way in which one idea turns towards or into another – and in doing so, creates an original expression to reflect this new or composite thought'.[16] In other words, tropes are the conventional means by which the poet makes innovative use of the existing structures of language, to permit new ideas and unexperienced feelings a new expression in the language. As Derek Attridge suggests, 'tropes are machinery which make possible the operation of inventiveness in the domain of meaning'.[17] They exist because, in Paterson's phrase, we are 'walking trope-generators', which is to say we must always generate wider meaning from the information we can gather 'in our perceptually reduced circumstances'.[18] We might usefully view the human condition itself as a kind of existential trope, a condition of metaphor or metonymy, 'depending on whether you regard your experience of the world as false or partial'.[19] To view it as accurate, however, as any reader who has paid sufficient attention to Paterson's disorienting and perceptually reimaginative poetry can attest, is not an option.

'The human trope' is what Paterson views as the 'symbolic accommodation' that defines the human dream.[20] But it is also the means by which language's function as a delimiting facilitator of human utility is turned against itself, the destabilising and alternative 'poetic function' of language that Paterson believes is poetry's raison d'être. 'Many of us have an inkling that this human dream is … false or partial, and take steps to correct it', he claims. 'This is the position occupied by human art, whose principal function is to join us to what we are not, and in doing so accomplish two beautifully contrastive things: restore something of the mystery of the wider world to our narrow human perception, and bring some of its hidden connections to light.'[21] As such, the skilled poet is able to manipulate our 'astonishing capacity for oversignifying, for "reading in"'[22] in order to create a new conceptual domain – that of the poem itself, which allows the profound linguistic articulation of a new idea or feeling.

'Two Trees' is one such poem, a narrative that appears to speak in strangely disguised metaphorical terms. It begins with the story of one 'Don Miguel', who wakes up one morning with the unbidden and novel idea of 'grafting his orange to his lemon tree' (*SP* 139). The process of doing so is painstaking: 'It took him the whole day to work them free', we are told, and even once they were lashed together, 'for twelve months, from the shame or from the fright / they put forth nothing'. Eventually, however, 'two lights' appeared in the tree's leaves, and over the years the two trees appeared as one, a 'magic tree' giving a 'double crop' (*SP* 139). This entire first stanza knowingly invites a particular metaphoric reading. In consisting of twelve full-rhymed lines of iambic pentameter – six couplets that almost appear to be missing a seventh, which would make for a variant sonnet – it encourages the reader to view Don Miguel's difficult but successful attempt to combine 'two trees' as a metaphor for poetic conception. Like the poet negotiating two different conceptual domains to produce new meaning and feeling through inventive use of extended metaphor, Don Miguel is engaged in making 'magic' out of two seemingly incompatible things. But where the reader might expect the final lines of the sonnet to make a happy conclusion of this successful imaginative enterprise, instead the stanza breaks into a second, offering a disturbing turn in its tale:

> The man who bought the house had had no dream
> so who can say what dark malicious whim
> led him to take his axe and split the bole
> along its fused seam, then dig two holes.
> And no, they did not die from solitude;
> nor did their branches bear a sterile fruit;
> nor did their unhealed flanks weep every spring
> for those four yards that lost them everything
> as each strained on its shackled root to face
> the other's empty, intricate embrace.

> They were trees, and trees don't weep or ache or shout.
> And trees are all this poem is about. (*SP* 139)

This second stanza cleverly shifts the metaphorical meaning we have been encouraged to develop in our reading of the first, simultaneously affirming it while denying it. When Don Miguel sells his house, the man who buys it has had 'no dream', implying he is not one engaged (nor even much interested) in the enterprise and imaginative efforts of the previous incumbent. He is not a poet or a reader, in other words, with a mind sensitive to the various ways of connecting and reimagining the world. The human dream, to which this 'man' appears to be beholden, is all, a sense of order he seems to want to re-impose when he separates and divides the magic tree on a 'malicious whim'. In this manner, the digging of 'two holes' not only refers literally to the act of separately replanting the trees, but figuratively suggests the everyday dead metaphors of the lemon tree and the orange tree, comfortably re-labelled and re-compartmentalised.

But this image of the dug hole also evokes, disconcertingly, a much more human burial. This is encouraged by the poem's insistent but deliberately unconvincing attempts to deny any kind of pathetic fallacy that we might impose on the separated trees. 'No, they did not die from solitude', the poem claims, second-guessing our meaning-making in typical Patersonian fashion, before ratcheting up the negatively defined emotional intensity: 'nor did their unhealed flanks weep every spring / for those four yards that lost them everything'. In the end, apparently, the trees are what they are: trees, and whatever human thoughts or feelings we might project onto them are simply the product of anthropocentric arrogance – something that the poem has manipulated, but for which, it is implied, we as readers are also responsible. And yet – the trees are *not* just trees, not in a poem that so clearly utilises them to affecting metaphorical ends. As A. E. Stallings notes of the speaker's emphatic but unconvincing dismissal:

> The denial rings both true and false – and hints at more pain than would a glib exploitation of trees as metaphor. Though he has invoked the human comparison only to reject it, the comparison remains invoked, like an unresolved dissonance throbbing in the air.[23]

The technique is one that exploits the way in which metaphor functions in order to assert a feeling so powerful it can often only be expressed indirectly: grief. As such, the two trees of the poem emerge as two separated lovers. Their painful parting is made more manageable for the lovelorn speaker by the metaphorical tale of the trees, which allows the poem to honour the initial 'magic' of their love, which 'over the years' got so 'tangled up' its force seemed to change the shape and texture of the very world around them: 'not one kid in the village' didn't know about it. But the metaphor also achieves the surprising effect of allowing the speaker both to deny his lingering feelings of anguish in the consequent break-up (insisting it is not a metaphor, but a purely literal story about two trees), while at the same time expressing and communicating something of that very anguish, in a poem that the poet knows, as well as reader, will be read as the extended metaphor it so clearly and affectingly is. If this sounds complicated, it is because the poem achieves these intellectually and emotionally transformative effects in a way that resists critical and analytical explanation. The poem's Machadian combination of difficult thought and feeling, through the medium of remarkably simple yet poetically charged language, conjures a precise sense of grief and loss that is without full articulation outside of the poem itself.

As one critic remarked: 'in *Rain*, what matters is children, friends, and work. But what also matters, it turns out, is matter, matter driven by the uncompromising laws of matter.'[24] The poems variously deal with complex personal negotiations and relationships – between lovers, the living and the dead, a poet and their work. But this emotive, everyday subject matter draws the reader into the poem only to give way to complex poetic-philosophical thinking – on the nature of human consciousness, forms both manmade and organic, and the mysterious forces governing the universe. Ever since *Nil Nil*'s 'The Ferryman's Arms', where the planetary alignment of balls on a pool table found that 'physics itself becomes something negotiable' (*SP* 3), the matter of the universe and our engagement with it has materialised as a recurrent interest throughout Paterson's oeuvre. In *Rain*, this interest has developed into an all-pervasive concern, not least given his by now heightened awareness of what he terms in *The Blind Eye* as 'the universal *defining* error of the doomed intelligence': the manner in which humankind has 'mistaken its dream for its element', divorcing the human and the natural (*BE* 120). As another critic has noted: 'That awareness of the viewing, thinking self is evident throughout *Rain*', a feature that illustrates how the book is primarily concerned 'with a kind of Platonic inquiry into the self and its relation to the physical world'.[25]

Perhaps the most avowedly philosophical poem in *Rain* is the 'The Day'. Here, Paterson makes resourceful use of the literary trope of metonymy, whereby a poem's imaginative suggestiveness within a given semantic category 'allows us to apply the same rule to many subjects in any arbitrarily law-governed context'.[26] This enables the poem to encourage the reader to extrapolate from its specific scenario towards wider truths about consciousness and the universe in which it finds itself. We will shortly address the purpose to which metonymy appears to be put in the poem, but first it is worth discussing the narrative tenor and argumentative trajectory that Paterson employs in 'The Day', and whereabouts this finds its origins.

'The Day' begins with a stark axiomatic statement, designed to immediately puncture any sentimentally religious view of the world: 'Life is no miracle' (*SP* 156). In this way, the poem sets out Paterson's stall, his brand of spiritually attuned scientific materialism locating wonder and mystery not in the alleged uniqueness of the human condition, but in the possibility that, rather than being 'chosen' by some unspecified and dubious deity, we are simply 'too far apart / to know ourselves the commonplace we are'. We are instead, the poem argues, 'as precious only as the gold in the sea: / nowhere and everywhere', a claim whose simile does not exactly refute the astonishing nature of human life, but sensibly suggests that in the incomprehensible vastness of the universe, or 'even in our own small galaxy', there is, in all possibility, life on another planet that we might recognise as such, were we ever able to access it.

Yet, of course, it is only through the human imagination, and the promise of perceptual transformation that the poem offers, that we can access this alien realm. 'So be assured', the poem encourages us, drawing the reader into its hypothetical yet suddenly tangible setting. If we choose to accept it, there is indeed 'another town' that, through the poem's deictic force, is much like that which anonymous narrator and reader find themselves, but one so distant that its 'today-light / won't reach a night of ours till Kirriemuir / is nothing but a vein of hematite' (*SP* 156). In familiar Patersonian style, it is the imaginative occasion of the poem that will serve to transcend the limitations of conventional human perception, asking us to entertain its intuitively reasoned scenario. And so the reader is presented with two alien creatures – 'say hairless, tall and dark, / but still as like ourselves as makes no odds' – who are 'pushing their wheeled contraptions through the park', in a town that appears as a mirror to a settlement in modern-day Scotland, but is in fact located on some immeasurably distant planet. Noting again the poem's title and its dedication *'for Maureen and Gus'*, we are invited to infer that these alien characters are the extraterrestrial equivalence to a newlywed couple here on Earth, who are presumably friends of the poet. On one level, the poem is an epithalamium. But it is also an occasion to meditate on intelligent life itself, and how connections between isolated consciousnesses must negotiate the vast gaps they are presented with – between intention and interpretation, perception and meaning, and across the physical realm of matter itself.

In the manner in which it proposes a scientific-materialist thesis and makes argument the engine of the poem, but also in its pared-back diction and natural speech rhythms framed by poetic form, 'The Day' recalls 'West-Running Brook', a poem by the American poet Robert Frost. Frost is undoubtedly a profound influence on Paterson's later work, and Paterson himself would doubtless credit 'West-Running Brook' as the rhetorical model for 'The Day'. In a lecture he gave entitled 'Frost as a Thinker', he presents Frost as a metaphysical and philosophical poet, who uses natural language to surprise the reader with complex ideas. This serves to align the American's work, both stylistically and thematically, with what we know to be Paterson's own aesthetic ambitions: the poem as brief, patterned, and original speech, a trustworthy piece of human discourse that is capable of proposing complex ideas in simple yet musically charged language, thus generating new meaning and knowledge in its dialogue with the reader. Speaking about 'West-Running Brook' in particular, Paterson argues it is a poem 'about getting your bearings in the whole cosmos … a semi-scientific polemic that is a quite explicit poem in its argument, but one that naturalises its rather austere thesis through the natural speech of its interlocutors'.[27] Here, it is not difficult to imagine that he could as well be talking about his own poem as about Frost's.

Having set its scene, most of 'The Day', like 'West-Running Brook', is given over to a playful, argumentative back-and-forth between the couple at its centre, who, 'sceptic of their laws and gods', are seen to make them 'witness to their given word' (*SP* 156). Whereas Frost's poem is a kind of humanist creation myth about human consciousness, however, finding its poetic symbol in the eponymous brook that flows west while all others flow east, 'trusting itself to go by contraries',[28] 'The Day' is much more concerned with the isolated nature of said consciousness, and those aforementioned gaps – between self and other, but also those across the vast stretches of the universe – which it must face. 'They talk, as we do now, of the Divide', the poem continues, as it brings human couple and alien couple, but also anonymous speaker and reader, into conversational alignment, before proposing that they 'set apart one minute of the day / to dream across the parsecs', in the hope of achieving a kind of 'cosmic solidarity' (*SP* 156). In this way, the poem offers up its ambitious aim: to not only find wonder, but also a measure of comfort, in a clear-eyed discussion about the immense body of impersonal, indifferent matter in which conscious emotional creatures such as ourselves find themselves situated.

The conversation that ensues between the couple is playful and at times entertainingly comic, but it is primarily one that takes its bearings with sad recognition. '"Think: all of us / as cut off as the living from the dead"', the husband proposes to his new wife, '"It's the size that's all wrong here. The emptiness"' (*SP* 157). For the husband, it is the fact that '"the biggest flashlight we could put together / is a match struck in the wind out here"' which is the source of existential distress, in the seemingly endless latticework of the universe. '"We're lost"', he wearily concludes, a statement that illustrates the poem's clever and repeated use of literary metonymy – or more specifically synecdoche, in which the part stands for the whole. For while the personal pronouns in 'The Day' refer to the plural 'we' of the couple engaged in their talk, they also refer to the anonymous narrator and reader, who are engaged in a not dissimilar process of collaborative meaning-making. Taking into account this inference and the poem's sweeping subject matter, the poem encourages us to interpret that plural 'we' as also referring to humankind in general, as well as possible variations on our form of conscious life dotted about the galaxies. The personal pronoun oscillates between the specific scenario of the poem, its illusion of a singular present moment, and the timeless and space-defying expanse of our combined perceptual experiences. Paterson's inventive manipulation of metonymy ensures that the poem is both an appealingly personal encounter between two lovers, as well as an all-encompassing, Rilkean philosophical enquiry into being itself.

It is impressive that the poem manages to be so emotionally affecting, in spite of the inevitable coldness of its philosophical focus. This is most apparent in the wife's replies to her husband, whose character she clearly understands and enjoys gently mocking, but also comforting. '"We talk, make love, we sleep in the same bed – but no matter what we do, you can't be me"', she states in po-faced fashion, knowingly encouraging her husband's bleak outlook: '"We only dream this place up in one head."' His reply, as anticipated, is even more despairing: '"Thanks for that … You're saying that because / the bed's a light-year wide, or might as well be, / I'm even lonelier than I thought I was?"' At this, the wife's tone softens, as she suggests that he has misunderstood her, and that our inventions of 'souls and gods and ghosts and afterlives' aren't a ploy to *bridge eternity*', but rather '"just the gap" – / she measures it – "from here to here"' (*SP* 157).

This instance of genuine and felt intimacy gives way to the final conclusion that one offers to the other, and that the poem offers to the reader: the only way to assuage the loneliness of the human situation is, as the wife suggests to her new husband, '"that you trust me with it *all*"'. In 'The Day' we find the suggestion that it is through love, the genuine connection of felt human intimacy, that we can transcend the isolated nature of the self. It is love, the poem proposes, that offers a defence against our apprehension of what another poem in *Rain*, 'Motive', labels that which 'hurries on its course / outside every human head' (*R* 39), which is to say the indifference of a godless and unfeeling universe. Consequently, 'The Day' alights on a note of powerful imaginative reconceptualisation that is also profoundly moving. The wedding rings that married couples exchange are not part of an empty tradition, it suggests, but a powerful metonym themselves, a symbol of the fact that *'even in this nothingness I found you; / I was lucky in the timing of my birth'* (*SP* 158).

Throughout this study we have seen how paradox and contradiction have come to define the poetic-philosophical arguments enacted by Paterson's verse. An especial paradoxical tension in Paterson's writing is that between presence and absence. *Rain* continues Paterson's project of interrogating the human dream, and its accompanying illusion of definitive, verifiable truth. The volume variously demonstrates, in coolly analytical yet also redemptive fashion, the ways in which the presence of meaning, thought, and emotion are in fact wholly absent from the world beyond our waking dream, projected by the mind and the eye into an indifferent universe. But if, as Dai George notes, 'opposed to this human eye is a larger metaphysical eye, an embodiment of the "void" underlying human life',[29] for the poet the challenge remains as to how the felt presence of human thought and emotion can successfully negotiate the absences that it must realistically face – a world without transcendental meaning, but also one in which all things eventually come to nothing, what Jan Schreiber describes as 'the bass note' of *Rain*: 'what we most love we must lose'.[30] As a means of enquiry, philosophy may long have been established on a purely intellectual footing, but as we have seen, for Paterson poetry is a unique mode of knowledge that requires the infusion of both thought and feeling. It is, at bottom, a more openly intuitive means of improvising truth, one that 'most fundamentally ... is just a couple of monkeys talking to each other'.[31]

With this is mind, the project of elegy in *Rain* is never solely one of commemorating the life of a friend or loved one who has departed. It is also a metaphysical enquiry into complex interrelations of presence and absence, as poetic-philosophical a subject matter as any other that the book's deeply reflective, perceptively interrogative poems address. 'The Swing' is one such poem, negotiating painful feelings of loss within a clear-eyed metaphysical apprehension of the nature of existence and reality. It begins innocuously, with the poet engaged in DIY handiwork:

The swing was picked up for the boys,
for the here-and-here-to-stay
and only she knew why it was
I dug so solemnly

I spread the feet two yards apart
and hammered down the pegs
filled up the holes and stamped the dirt
around its skinny legs (*SP* 141)

These quatrains open the poem with the kind of everyday quotidian setting that, given the manner in which Paterson's verse serves to estrange the ordinary in imaginative ways, should prepare the reader for a perceptual transformation of their subject matter. The lines hint at unspoken absence and painful regret: not only is the speaker found digging 'solemnly', his sons, 'the boys', are described as 'the here-and-here-to-stay', a peculiar definition of their existential presence that begs the question as to what precisely *isn't* here to stay. These mysterious details draw our attention alongside the plain sense of the poem, which is to say the swing and its construction, which supplies the poem's central focus and what T. S. Eliot would call its 'objective correlative'.

For Eliot, the 'objective correlative' is the only means of expressing emotion in art. It functions by finding 'a set of objects, a situation, a chain of events which shall be the formula of that particular emotion'.[32] Michael Donaghy suggests a revised version of the concept in his essay 'Wallflowers', in which he discusses how

> modern poets often build their poems about a single point of emotional focus analogous to a point of optical focus in photographs – often represented by a single object held, like Yorick's skull, in the poet's hand, a magician's prop toward which we direct our attention so that the magic can proceed by sleight of hand.[33]

Just as we have seen how the trees in 'Two Trees' cannot simply be considered as trees alone, the swing in 'The Swing' is not merely what it seems. Paterson is acutely aware of the ways in which any poem invites the reader to *read in*, allowing the poem to productively oversignify. In 'The Swing' this is no different, though the poet-speaker also appears to occupy this readerly position himself, comprehending the 'poem' of the swing as a representation of something else. As such, having 'fixed the yellow seat', he stands back to admire his work, but instead sees its 'frail trapeze' as a haunting symbol of 'the child that would not come / of what we knew had two more days / before we sent it home' (*SP* 141). Suddenly, the painful emotional subtext of the poem hits us: there will be an abortion.

Like the unassuaged, almost unspeakable grief in 'Two Trees', 'The Swing' harbours a metaphoric truth that the poet-speaker can only attempt to deny: 'I know that there is nothing here / no venue and no host'. In trying to reassure the reader as much as himself, the speaker claims it is 'the honest fulcrum of the hour / that engineers our ghost', which is to say that the occasion of building the swing, its centrality, has made it into a vessel for the unassuaged feelings that he harbours: the 'ghost' of the unborn, and soon-to-be terminated, child. However the poet tries to convince himself that 'the bright sweep' of the swing's 'radar-arc' is simply 'the human dream / handing us from dark to dark', from one state of unknowing to another, he cannot see the swing as anything other than a physical representation of the aborted child, and the terrible weight of his feelings about it. 'For all the coldness of his creed', he cannot 'weigh the ghosts we are / against those we deliver' (*SP* 142). In the end, the intense knowledge that comes from philosophical meditation, from piercing enquiries into the nature of self and other – the understanding that poetry itself has brought to the speaker – is of little use or comfort in the face of death and grief.

Lost and bereft, all the poet-speaker can do is give 'the empty seat a push', an act that is quietly heart-breaking, and supplies the poem with a profound emotional force. But it also serves to bring the speaker (and poet and reader) some unexpected relief, as 'nothing made a sound / and swung between two skies to brush / her feet upon the ground'. As one critic has noted, 'the paradox behind that simple-seeming phrase, "nothing made a sound", can be read two ways – is there no sound, or is there a sound that is made by "nothing"?'[34] This duality of meaning is one that, from one angle, delivers the poem's painful emotional resonance, but from another, also supplies us with a sense of poetry's ability to briefly transcend death. In this sense, the poem has indeed made a 'sound' out of 'nothing': its lyric song has transformed the absence of the child into a powerfully felt presence. As such, 'The Swing' is a tenderly expressed leave-taking, but it is also a portrayal of poetry's ability to remake a painfully real absence into a lasting presence. This is the case even as it is inevitably confined to the poem's conjured illusion of the present moment, given the way in which 'time is a little collapsed into no-time, as we lose some sense of its passing' (O 69).

Rain comes to a close with its title poem. A songful paean to the speaker's love of 'all films that start with rain', it claims that any cinematic piece incorporating this atmospheric feature serves to absolve it of unintentionally comic deficiencies in plot, characterisation, and performance (*SP* 168). 'However bad or overlong', the poem announces, 'such a film can do no wrong'. This is because, we discover, the poet *reads in* to the rain, much as we found the speaker in 'The Swing' did, and much as the poems in *Rain* illustrate what readers cannot help but do time and again, in embracing art's productive over-signification. As such, 'Rain' offers up an interpretation of the rain as a kind of post-religious absolution, a cleansing of all the grief, pain, effort, and suffering that any attempt to perfect life or art necessarily invites:

> *forget the ink, the milk, the blood –*
> *all was washed clean with the flood*
> *we rose up from the falling waters*
> *the fallen rain's own sons and daughters*
>
> *and none of this, none of this matters.* (SP 169)

In a radio interview, it was suggested to Paterson that 'it sounds like you've taken yourself out of religion, but religion hasn't taken itself out of you'.[35] His reply was that this was 'a terrifying thought', before he went on to state: 'If you believe yourself to be infected with original sin, then why wouldn't you want shot of it? Why wouldn't you want to consider it a construct? Of course you would.'[36] At this, the interviewer suggests that, rather than being a 'theoretical and cultural' aspect of 'the Scottish soul' as Paterson proposes, it is one that is in fact part of his personal 'DNA'. 'Well, that's the worry isn't it', Paterson replies: 'if it's all from mother's milk, there's nothing to be done, the game's over'.[37] It is at this point the interviewer arrives at the critical revelation: 'Maybe there is nothing to be done, maybe it's out of the fact there's nothing to be done that you make the poetry.'

Paterson cannot help but agree. If *Rain* is a collection that illustrates the many successes of his refinement of poetry as a unique mode of knowledge, it also knowingly highlights the inevitable failures of the art form. Like any means of intellectual enquiry, it cannot hope to permanently release us from ongoing struggles between self and other. But as we have seen throughout our discussions of Paterson's work, what separates poetry from other forms of knowledge is its ability to place the larger conceptual domain of the human dream – which is to say the 'blind tyranny' of our habituated perspective[38] – under linguistic challenge and interrogation. As *Rain* shows, the poet who recognises this can make the poem into a site for highly memorable new meaning-making. In the merging of sound and sense, and in brief, patterned, and original speech, the poems of *Rain* therefore argue that poetry can, in small but significant ways, remake reality itself. This is the truest meaning of poetry as a mode of knowledge.

Coda:
40 Sonnets (2015)
and *Zonal* (2020)

In illustrating the considerable stylistic developments of Paterson's poetry, alongside the ways in which his work distinguishes verse as a unique mode of knowledge, this study appears to find itself in broad agreement with Sean O'Brien's suggestion that 'few poets can have covered as much ground in twenty years as Don Paterson'.[1] The chronological nature of this study will, I hope, have allowed readers both familiar with and new to this major poet's work to gain a fuller appreciation of its singular development, from the precocious promise of *Nil Nil*, through to the magnum opus of *Rain*. Given the poetry's remarkable imaginative reach, tonal range, and musical memorability, but also its self-reflecting capacities, its reflexive commentaries on poetry itself, and its poetic-philosophical enquiries into the nature of the human condition, Paterson surely now ranks among the most significant English-language poets currently writing.

Rain presents Paterson's most accomplished and ambitious work to date. As the then Poet Laureate Carol Ann Duffy remarked on its publication: 'To read this book is to have the privilege of seeing a world-class talent assert itself, as Seamus Heaney did with *North*.'[2] The book's poems extend previous developments in Paterson's oeuvre – particularly the manner in which the Rilkean versions in *Orpheus* gave license to be both prophetic and more explicitly philosophical – to produce a full enactment of Paterson's sense of poetry as a unique means of intellectual enquiry. In poems that exploit the literary tropes of metaphor and metonymy in innovative ways, *Rain* emerges, under critical scrutiny, as a collection that not only uncovers poetry as 'the reflexive turn language makes against its own project of conceptual division',[3] but one that also manages, through the imperative of its elegiac project, to fully combine the emotive, the spiritual, and the compassionate with the shrewdly philosophical approach of a materialist outlook, one that 'doesn't make the world any less wonderful ... but does afford a more distant perspective ... on human affairs, petty kinds of struggle'.[4]

Paterson's achievement in *Rain* is to have produced poems that serve to distinguish poetry from other modes of enquiry, including science and philosophy, as a distinctive mode of knowledge. In doing so, the book sets his work apart from that of his contemporaries. Poetry, through Paterson's particular example, requires the infusion of both thought and feeling, providing a more openly intuitive means of improvising truth. Not only does it make the reader 'excited, open to suggestion, vulnerable to reprogramming',[5] but in repeatedly exposing the ways in which '"we only dream this place up in one head"' (*SP* 157) – which is to say, how reality is shaped by the neural computation of sense data and the compartmentalising functions of language 'nailing down the human dream'[6] – it serves to make poetry into a site for remaking that very reality, offering renewed understanding and generating new knowledge.

Having achieved this, and given the diverse adaptability that is his work's stylistic hallmark, Paterson's poetry has since taken a characteristically unpredictable turn. At the same time, these more recent poems also return to forms and themes that will be familiar to Paterson readers. A seventh volume, *40 Sonnets*, demonstrates perhaps the poet's fullest exploration of a form that has long fascinated him, having previously delivered some of his strongest beliefs and convictions about the art form in general, and having generated some of his most rewarding poems. From *Nil Nil* with its studies in desolation and aftermath, to the serious play with personae in *God's Gift to Women* and the existential hymns for the poet's twin sons in *Landing Light*, the sonnet abounds throughout Paterson's oeuvre. Nowhere more so than in *Orpheus*, where it proved crucial in Paterson's stylistic development, given its specific formal shaping. In negotiating between the spirit of Rilke's originals and the imperative of lyric unity, the infusion of sound and sense emerges as the guiding principle behind Paterson's composition of the lyric poem. Rilke also enabled him to illustrate his sense of the sonnet form as an evolutionary necessity, as his highly musical mnemonic versions propose the way in which the 'uniquely human business' of song[7] can offer 'a stay against time's passing' (O 69).

At a relatively early stage in his career as poet and commentator, however, Paterson had already showcased the sonnet's rich history in editing a popular anthology. The longevity of *101 Sonnets: From Shakespeare to Heaney* (1999) has had as much to do with the range of sonnets it contains as its entertaining and deeply thoughtful introduction. Even then, the poet could be found arguing for the sonnet as 'one of the greatest achievements of human ingenuity', a 'box for dreams' that 'represents one of the most characteristic shapes human thought can take'.[8] Whatever an individual reader makes of his thesis, it remains compelling, grounded in the unifying and sense-making powers of rhyme and metre, the sonnet's loose adherence to the proportions of the golden section, and his deep admiration for what the best sonneteers can do with this little 'squared circle', a resistant medium that allows poets to 'trick a logic from the shadows' of unconscious thought.[9] Much like his layman's guide *Reading Shakespeare's Sonnets* (2010), it is a fascinating but also original work, not least given his interest is also that of the accomplished practitioner.

In this sense, a collection comprising fourteen-liners should not have come as a surprise. Moreover, after the austere undertaking of *Rain*, Paterson must have been on the lookout, in a practical sense as much as any other, for a more various way back into writing verse. In *40 Sonnets*, Paterson sets about illustrating the form's versatility, but also its enduring appeal. Delivering exactly what it promises, it is an especially slight collection, even from an author known for championing brevity. Where many of his contemporaries exhibit a trend towards publishing collections of poetry that far surpass *40 Sonnets* in length, however, Paterson's icy intelligence, imagination, and painstaking craft make for disproportionately substantial reading:

I must quit sleeping in the afternoon.
I do it for my heart, but all too soon
my heart has called it off. It does not love me.
If it downed tools, there'd soon be nothing of me.
Its hammer-beat says *you are*, not *I am*.
It prints me off here like a telegram.
What do *I* say? How can the lonely word
know who has sent it out, or who has heard? (*40S* 3)

From the everyday setting of an afternoon nap to intimations of mortality, the book's opening poem, 'Here', offers a fully Patersonian meditation on identity as linguistic gesture. It is delivered in crisp and exact language, with heart-thumping end rhymes that feel natural and unforced. As we have seen, it is this command of poetry's musicality combined with lucid philosophical thinking that has come to define Paterson's poetry. A familiar spirit of questing and questioning makes for some of the most memorable and accomplished sonnets in the collection. 'Souls', for instance, takes the numinous aspects of our selves and expresses them as an aberration from the physical, a world where 'space is stone, and time a breackneck terror' (*40S* 42), while in 'The Air', the element we take for granted becomes a mysterious abstraction, 'an empty datastream' that is 'nowhere' and 'never', a powerful reminder that we are but a brief chapter in the universe's narrative (*40S* 5). It is poems such as these that have raised Paterson's stature to that of one of the most significant English-language poets currently writing. If they might sometimes exhibit a slight over-earnestness, and wear their author's European influences too heavily for certain contemporary tastes (both Antonio Machado and Rainer Maria Rilke remain as lingering presences), they fully demonstrate the rare value of a poetry of assertion and argument. Poetry as a mode of knowledge, no less.

However, unlike the unwavering focus of *Rain*'s exacting bleakness, it is the stylistic, thematic, and tonal variety of *40 Sonnets* that comes to define the volume, presenting a bravura performance. Picking up where *Landing Light*'s 'Waking with Russell' and 'The Thread' left off in their meditative approach to fatherhood, 'The Roundabout' is perhaps the most beautiful of Paterson's poems to his twin sons, finding poet-speaker looking up 'at a sky so clear / there was nothing in the world to prove our turning' (*40S* 44). Elsewhere, 'Requests' and 'To Dundee City Council' offer fine examples of Paterson's cutting poetic humour: both are damning indictments of the artless and inept, the former addressed to a blathering poet on stage, the latter to a council presiding over a local library where 'poor folks go to die / or download porno on the free wifi' (*40S* 28). In stark contrast, 'Funeral Prayer' is a warm, frank yet simple elegy that one can imagine being read at many an actual service (*40S* 14), while 'Mercies', the tale of having a beloved pet put down, similarly evinces and continues Paterson's unfashionable sense of poetry as a moral project, intent on connecting with readers through precise language in order to communicate deeply complex emotion (*40S* 43). As a slender book of surprising emotional, intellectual, and tonal range, *40 Sonnets* ultimately cements Paterson's standing as a poet who shows that poetic form is precisely what you make of it. As William Boyd has claimed, the book 'breathes vivacity into an ancient format, showing that poetic structures are no impediment to emotional intensity'.[10]

At the time of writing, Paterson's eighth volume of poems, *Zonal*, has only recently appeared, billed as an 'experiment in science fiction and fantastic autobiography'. It advances Paterson's keen sense of poetry's artifice – especially its trick of conjuring coherent, real, and seemingly present speakers – put to characteristically serious yet playful ends. Initial critical responses have observed that the volume's long and loosely metrical lines represent something of a stylistic departure for a poet hitherto known for deftly combining the rhythms of everyday speech with exacting formal structure. But as one critic has remarked, 'the subject matter of *Zonal* indicates that Paterson is still playing the same high-stakes thematic games, writing about "death, doubles and the void", to use his own words'.[11] 'Don't think for a second that Death loves his work', states the speaker in the volume's opening narrative, relating a parable in which a self-deceiving salesman tries to buy off the grim reaper (Z 9). In 'Lazarus', what initially looks like a comic retelling of the Biblical tale as opportunity for self-improvement soon meets an altogether darker, distinctly Orphic contemplation of the void: 'a dead man walking was a grand thing to be if you'd already died: alive, but done with the fear of death' (Z 68). However imaginative and inventive the various poetic strategies he employs, it seems that Paterson is always destined to return to those fundamental thematic concerns that, as we have seen, dominate and define his oeuvre to date.

This study can only really end on that speculative note, but whatever path Paterson's poetry takes in the future, it will likely be an unexpected and rewarding one, for poet and reader alike. As the poet himself states in *How Poets Work*:

> I'm terrified of repeating myself, and have evolved various strategies to try and counter this – well one, really: keep altering the strategy. The great danger, for me, is to continue to mine a seam long after it's yielded up the last diamond ... after a while, you're not even bringing up coal anymore, just dirt ... but now there's a tiny village near the pithead, with a grocer's and a sub-post office, and it's twinned with some crap sonnet sequence in Normandy; and as laird of the estate, you're often the last person to admit it's no longer a viable concern. So I've evolved this rather daft solution, which obviously has its own hazards; I'll try and mine tin one week, uranium the next, jade the week after, and so on ... I'd hate to think I was writing the same poem twice. I like the idea of the poem as a self-contained universe, the national anthem of a wee vernacular Atlantis whose laws, customs, geography and weather could all be derived from its close study.[12]

Notes

PROLOGUE

1. Dai George, 'Degrees of Sight', *Boston Review* (September 9, 2010), <http://www.bostonreview.net/george-degrees-of-sight> [accessed April 2020].
2. Edna Longley, *The Bloodaxe Book of 20th Century Poetry* (Tarset, Northumberland: Bloodaxe, 2000), 363.
3. A. S. Byatt, comment included on the paperback edition of Don Paterson's *Landing Light* (London: Faber, 2004).
4. Paul Muldoon, comment included on the paperback edition of Don Paterson's *Rain* (London: Faber, 2010).
5. Sean O'Brien, 'Don Paterson: *Rain*, Etc', *Poetry Review*, 99:4 (Winter 2009), 61.
6. Don Paterson, 'The Dilemma of the Peot [*sic*]', *How Poets Work*, ed. Tony Curtis (Bridgend, Wales: Seren, 1996), 155.
7. The *via negativa* – Latin for 'negative way', also known as apophatic theology – is a theology that attempts to describe the divine by negation; it speaks only in terms of what may *not* be said about God in an attempt to understand what He is. In Chapter 3 this concept, and Paterson's unique poetic-philosophical adaptation of it, will be outlined and discussed in further detail.
8. Jorge Luis Borges, 'Borges and I', *Labyrinths*, trans. by James E. Irby (London: Penguin, 1970), 283.
9. Antonio Porchia, *Voices*, trans. by W. S. Merwin (Washington: Copper Canyon Press, 2003), 101.
10. T. S. Eliot, 'Tradition and the Individual Talent', *The Sacred Wood* (1920; London: Faber, 1997), 44.
11. Ibid.
12. Paterson, *The Poem: Lyric, Sign, Metre* (London: Faber, 2018), 11.
13. Paterson, 'Leading Light', an interview with Nicholas Wroe, *The Guardian* (November 25, 2006), <http://www.guardian.co.uk/books/2006/nov/25/featuresreviews.guardianreview7> [accessed May 2020].
14. Ibid.

15. Ibid.
16. Paterson, *The Poem: Lyric, Sign, Metre*, 14.
17. Ibid.
18. Ibid., 13.
19. Charles Simic, cited in Paterson, 'Fourteen Notes on the Version', *Orpheus: A Version of Rilke's* Die Sonette an Orpheus (London: Faber, 2006), 75.
20. Alan Gillis, 'Don Paterson', *The Edinburgh Companion to Contemporary Scottish Poetry*, eds Matt McGuire and Colin Nicholson (Edinburgh: Edinburgh University Press, 2009), 186.
21. Ibid., 175.
22. O'Brien, 72.
23. Victor Shklovsky, 'Art as Technique', *Russian Formalist Criticism: Four Essays*, ed. and trans. by Lee T. Lemon and Marion J. Reis (Lincoln, NE: University of Nebraska Press, 1965), 12.
24. Paterson, 'The Dark Art of Poetry', T. S. Eliot Lecture (October 30, 2004), reproduced in *The Guardian* (November 6, 2004), <https://www.theguardian.com/books/poetry/features/0,12887,1344654,00.html> [accessed May 2020].
25. Paterson, 'Introduction', *New British Poetry*, ed. with Charles Simic (Minneapolis: Graywolf Press, 2004), xxv.
26. Ibid., xxxiii.
27. John Keats, 'On the Aims of Poetry: Letter to J. H. Reynolds, 3 February 1818', <http://www.poetryfoundation.org/learning/essay/237836?page=2> [accessed April 2020].
28. Paterson, in 'Private Enterprise for the Public Good: John Stammers Interviews Don Paterson', *Magma*, 12 (Spring 1998), <http://poetrymagazines.org.uk/magazine/recordcae4.html?id=3524> [accessed April 2020].
29. Gillis, 175.
30. O'Brien, 62.
31. Crotty, 'Between Home and Rome', *Times Literary Supplement* (December 12, 2003), 5.
32. Michael Wood, 'Other Ways to Leave the Room', *London Review of Books*, 21:23 (November 25, 1999), 25–6.
33. Robert Crawford, 'Deep Down in the Trash', *London Review of Books*, 19:16 (August 21, 1997), 26.
34. O'Brien, 63.
35. Stéphane Mallarmé, letter to Henri Cazalis (April 1866), *Selected Letters of Stéphane Mallarmé*, ed. and trans. by Rosemary Lloyd (Chicago: University of Chicago Press, 1988), 60.
36. Dan Chiasson, 'Forms of Attention', *The New Yorker* (April 19, 2010), 116.

CHAPTER 1: FOR THE HELL OF IT: *NIL NIL* (1993)

1. Gillis, 173.
2. Ibid., 175.
3. Louis MacNeice, 'Charon', *Collected Poems*, ed. Peter McDonald (London: Faber, 2007), 593.
4. 'To begin thinking about time, we might / take all the verbs we like to think we do // to time, and turn those verbs on us, and say / that times wastes us, and time saves and buys us, / that time spends us, and time marks and kills us.' William Matthews, 'Time', *Time and Money* (New York: Houghton Mifflin, 1995), 14.
5. Gillis, 175.
6. Ibid., 174.
7. Edward Thomas, 'The Other', *Collected Poems* (London: Faber, 2004), 12.
8. W. B. Yeats, 'Anima Hominis', *Per Amica Silentia Lunae* (Norwood: Norwood Press/The Macmillan Company, 1918), 29.
9. Jean Moréas, 'Le Manifeste du Symbolisme', *Le Figaro* (September 18, 1886), <http://www.ieeff.org/manifestesymbolisme.htm> [accessed April 2020].
10. Timothy Donnelly, 'Nothing, in Other Words: On the Poetry of Don Paterson', *Verse*, 20:2/3 (2004), <http://www.cstone.net/~poems/essadonn.htm> [accessed April 2020].
11. Sarah Broom, *Contemporary British and Irish Poetry* (Basingstoke: Palgrave MacMillan, 2006), 35.
12. Vicki Bertram, *Gendering Poetry: Contemporary Women and Men Poets* (London: Pandora Press, 2005), 188.
13. Gillis, 178.
14. Ian Sansom, 'Excess Its Own Reward', *Poetry Review*, 87:2 (Summer 1997), 44.
15. Adam Thorpe, 'Antiseptic Sceptics', *The Observer* (August 29, 1993), 53.
16. Seamus Heaney, 'Digging', *Death of a Naturalist* (1966; London: Faber, 1999), 3–4.
17. Broom, 34.
18. Heaney, 'Digging', *Death of a Naturalist*, 3.
19. Gillis, 178.
20. Broom, 34.
21. Paterson, in 'Private Enterprise for the Public Good: John Stammers Interviews Don Paterson', *Magma*, 12 (Spring 1998).
22. Jorge Luis Borges, 'Borges and I', *Labyrinths*, trans. by James E. Irby (London: Penguin, 1970), 283.
23. Gillis, 178.
24. Paterson, in Raymond Friel's 'Don Paterson, Interviewed', *Talking*

Verse, eds Robert Crawford, Henry Hart, David Kinloch, and Richard Price (St Andrews: Verse, 1995), 193.

25. Gillis, 178.
26. Ibid.
27. Paterson, 'The Dark Art of Poetry: T. S. Eliot Lecture, 2004'.
28. Adolf Zeising, trans. in Richard Padovan, *Proportion: Science, Philosophy, Architecture* (London: Taylor & Francis, 1999), 306.
29. George Markowsky, 'Misconceptions about the Golden Ratio', *College Mathematics Journal*, 23:1 (January 1992), 2.
30. Entropy may be defined as the tendency exhibited by thermo-dynamic systems – which is to say, all things – towards disorder and chaos, as well as the process that leads to this. The concept is best understood in relation to the second law of thermodynamics, which the German physicist Rudolf Clausius (1822–88), who proposed the first mathematical version of entropy, summarised as follows: 'The entropy of the universe tends to a maximum.' In essence, while the world appears to the naked human eye in its narrow and habitual guise of a vast collection of apparently solid objects, it is in fact always evolving towards thermodynamic equilibrium, and the eventual complete absence of form and shape. The ramifications of this concept can be seen to underpin Paterson's poem 'Next to Nothing', but also *Nil Nil* as a collection.
31. Porchia, *Voices*, 33.
32. Ibid.
33. Crotty, 5.
34. To clarify: this scientific hypothesis is essentially an extension of the concept of entropy already discussed, as determined by the second law of thermodynamics. The theory proposes that, given entropy, the universe will eventually reach a state in which there is no thermodynamic free energy; hence it will no longer be able to sustain any processes that consume energy. In discussions of the ultimate fate of the universe, this theory is usually referred to as the 'heat death' hypothesis, attributed to the mathematician, physicist, and engineer William Thomson, 1st Baron Kelvin.

CHAPTER 2: WHICH MAN I AM: *GOD'S GIFT TO WOMEN* (1997)

1. Bertram, 193.
2. Peter Robinson, *Twentieth Century Poetry: Selves and Situations* (Oxford: Oxford University Press, 2005), 6–7 [my italics].
3. Paterson, 'Introduction', *New British Poetry*, xxx.

4. Paterson, in 'Private Enterprise for the Public Good: John Stammers Interviews Don Paterson', *Magma*, 12 (Spring 1998).

5. William Scammell, 'I'll See You in Church, Jimmy', *The Independent* (May 4, 1997), 38.

6. Conor O'Callaghan, 'Al Dente', *Metre*, 3 (Autumn 1997), 40–2.

7. Keith Bruce, 'Inspiration from his Own Law', *The Glasgow Herald* (May 3, 1997), 12.

8. Robert Potts, 'Reflected Glare', *Times Literary Supplement* (September 12, 1997), 21.

9. Scammell, 38.

10. Eliot, 'Tradition and the Individual Talent', *The Sacred Wood*, 41.

11. Ibid., 44.

12. Ibid., 48–9.

13. Paterson, in Raymond Friel's 'Don Paterson, Interviewed', *Talking Verse*, 194.

14. Eliot, 'Tradition and the Individual Talent', *The Sacred Wood*, 49.

15. Ibid., 48.

16. Maud Ellman, *The Poetics of Impersonality* (Brighton: Harvester Press, 1987), ix.

17. Abbas Ibn Al-Ahnaf, *Birds Through an Alabaster Ceiling: Three Abyssinian Poets – Arab Poetry of the Abbasid Period*, trans. by G. B. H. Wightman Abudlla Udhari, and A. Y. Al-Udhari (Harmondsworth: Penguin, 1975), 36.

18. Paterson, 'The Dark Art of Poetry: T.S. Eliot Lecture, 2004'.

19. John Keats, 'This Living Hand, Now Warm and Capable', *Selected Poems* (1819; London: Penguin, 2007), 237.

20. Stéphane Mallarmé, 'Crise de Vers', *La Revue Blanche* (September, 1895); trans. by Rosemary Lloyd in *Mallarmé: The Poet and his Circle* (Ithaca, NY: Cornell University Press, 1999), 55.

21. Mallarmé, letter to Eugène Lefébure, February 1865, in *Selected Letters of Stéphane Mallarmé*, trans. by Rosemary Lloyd (Chicago: University of Chicago Press, 1988), 48.

22. Roland Barthes, 'The Death of the Author', *Image – Music – Text*, trans. by Stephen Heath (London: Fontana, 1977), 143.

23. Paterson, 'The Dilemma of the Peot [*sic*]', *How Poets Work*, 155.

24. Michael Wood, 'Other Ways to Leave the Room', *London Review of Books*, 21:23 (November 25, 1999), 26.

25. Robert Crawford, 'Deep Down in the Trash', *London Review of Books*, 19:16 (August 21, 1997), 26.

26. Bertram, 189.

27. Ibid., 188.

28. John Donne, 'Community', *The Complete English Poems* (1971; London: Penguin, 1996), 48.

29. Judith Butler, *Gender Trouble: Feminism and the Subversion of Identity* (London: Routledge, 1990), 136.

30. Ibid., vii.

31. Ibid., 139.

32. O'Brien, 'Don Paterson: *Rain*, Etc', *Poetry Review*, 64.

33. Paterson, 'The Dilemma of the Peot [*sic*]', *How Poets Work*, 157.

34. Paterson, 'Leading Light', interview with Nicholas Wroe, *The Guardian* (November 25, 2006), <http://www.guardian.co.uk/books/2006/nov/25/featuresreviews.guardianreview7> [accessed May 2020].

35. John Donne, 'To Sir Edward Herbert, at Juliers', *The Complete English Poems*, 218–19.

36. Crawford, 'Deep Down in the Trash', *London Review of Books*, 26.

CHAPTER 3: NOT YOUR NAME, NOT MINE: *THE EYES* (1999)

1. Peter Forbes, Introduction to Paterson's work in 'Seven Years On: The New Generation', *Poetry Review*, 101:1 (Spring 2001), 7.

2. John Burnside, 'Spanish Eyes', *Poetry Review*, 89:3 (Autumn 1999), 71.

3. Ibid., 70–1.

4. Alan S. Trueblood, Introduction to *Antonio Machado: Selected Poems*, trans. by Alan S. Trueblood (1982; Cambridge, MA: Harvard University Press, 2003), 17.

5. Paterson, in Marco Fazzini's 'Interview with Don Paterson', 2009, 7, <http://www.donpaterson.com/files/interview1.htm> [accessed April 2020].

6. Jamie McKendrick, 'The Player of Zero-sum Games', *Times Literary Supplement* (January 14, 2000), 31.

7. Mallarmé, 'Crise de Vers', *La Revue Blanche*; trans. by Rosemary Lloyd in *Mallarmé*, 55.

8. Trueblood, Introduction to *Antonio Machado: Selected Poems*, 39.

9. Ibid., 14–15.

10. A direct crib from the original Spanish of 'Parábolas: IV Consejos' reads as follows:

> Be happy to wait, and wait for the tide to flow –
> a beached boat doesn't worry about waiting.
> If you wait, and look, then victory is yours,
> since life is long and art simply a toy.
> And if life is short
> and the sea doesn't reach your little boat,
> go on waiting, without worry or expectation,
> for art is long and, besides, it does not matter.

11. Trueblood, 'Parables: IV Advice', *Antonio Machado: Selected Poems*, 149.

12. Porchia, *Voices*, 63.
13. W. S. Merwin, 'A Note on Antonio Porchia', *Voices*, ix.
14. William Wordsworth, Preface of 1800, with a collation of the enlarged preface of 1802, in *Lyrical Ballads*, ed. W. J. B. Owen (Oxford: Oxford University Press, 1969), 173.
15. Machado, *Obras. Poesia y prosa*, eds Aurora de Albornoz and Guillermo de Torre (Buenos Aires: Losada, 1964), 714.
16. Trueblood, Introduction to *Antonio Machado: Selected Poems*, 40–1.
17. Thanissaro Bhikkhu (trans.), '35.85: Suñña Sutta: Empty', *Samyutta Nikaya*, <http://www.accesstoinsight.org/tipitaka/sn/sn35/sn35.085.than.html> [accessed April 2020].
18. Michael Wood, 'Other Ways to Leave the Room', *London Review of Books*, 21:23 (November 25, 1999), 25–6.
19. Eliot, 'The Metaphysical Poets', *Homage to John Dryden: Three Essays on Poetry of the Seventeenth Century*, in *The Hogarth Essays*, 218.
20. McKendrick, 'The Player of Zero-sum Games', *Times Literary Supplement*, 31.
21. Eliot, 'The Metaphysical Poets', *Homage to John Dryden: Three Essays on Poetry of the Seventeenth Century*, in *The Hogarth Essays*, 218.
22. Robert Bly, 'A Few Notes on Antonio Machado', *Times Alone: Selected Poems of Antonio Machado*, trans. by Robert Bly (Middletown, CT: Wesleyan University Press, 1983), 2.
23. Bly, 'A Few Notes on Antonio Machado', *Times Alone: Selected Poems of Antonio Machado*, 4.
24. Trueblood, 'The Eyes', *Antonio Machado: Selected Poems*, 205–6.
25. William Scammell, 'Like Guitar Music Transcribed for the Piano', *The Independent* (February 20, 2000), 13.
26. Machado, *Juan de Mairena*, ed. J. M. Valverde (Madrid: Castalia, 1971), 172.
27. Trueblood, Introduction to *Antonio Machado: Selected Poems*, 14.
28. Ibid., 32.
29. Paterson, in Marco Fazzini's 'Interview with Don Paterson', 12.
30. Trueblood, 'Parables: V Profession of Faith', *Antonio Machado: Selected Poems*, 149.
31. Paterson, in Marco Fazzini's 'Interview with Don Paterson', 9.
32. Paterson, 'The Dark Art of Poetry: T.S. Eliot Lecture, 2004'.
33. Emil Cioran, 'The Parasite of Poets', *A Short History of Decay* (1949; London: Penguin, 2010), 103–4.
34. Trueblood, Introduction to *Antonio Machado: Selected Poems*, 61.
35. Ibid., 17.
36. Wood, 'Other Ways to Leave the Room', *London Review of Books*, 25–6.
37. Machado, cited in Bly, *Times Alone: Selected Poems of Antonio Machado*, 79–80.

CHAPTER 4: SHREWD OBLIQUITY OF SPEECH:
LANDING LIGHT (2003)

1. Bernard O'Donoghue, 'Dante's Peak', *The Independent* (September 27, 2003), 38.
2. O'Brien, 'Don Paterson: *Rain*, Etc', *Poetry Review*, 66.
3. Broom, 35.
4. Natalie Pollard, 'Don Paterson: On the Money', *Speaking to You: Contemporary Poetry and Public Address* (Oxford: Oxford University Press, 2012), 221–2.
5. Adam Newey, 'Flints and Sparks', *The Guardian* (November 15, 2003).
6. Pollard, 218.
7. Keith Green, 'Deixis and the Poetic Persona', *The Language and Literature Reader*, eds Ronald Carter and Peter Stockwell (Abingdon: Routledge, 2008), 127.
8. Ibid., 130.
9. Ibid., 135.
10. Pollard, 217.
11. Ibid., 218.
12. Michael Donaghy, 'Wallflowers: A Lecture on Poetry with Misplaced Notes and Additional Heckling', *The Shape of the Dance: Essays, Interviews and Digressions*, eds Adam O'Riordan and Maddy Paxman (London: Picador, 2009), 4.
13. Paterson, *The Poem: Lyric, Sign, Metre*, 9–10.
14. Peter Howarth, 'Degree of Famousness etc', *London Review of Books*, 35:6 (March 21, 2013), 31.
15. Ruth Bienstock Anolik, 'Introduction: The Dark Unknown', *The Gothic Other: Racial and Social Constructions in the Literary Imagination*, eds Ruth Bienstock Anolik and Douglas L. Howard (North Carolina: McFarland, 2004), 1.
16. Ibid.
17. Alison Milbank, 'Gothic Fiction Tells us the Truth about our Divided Nature', *The Guardian* (November 27, 2011), <http://www.theguardian.com/commentisfree/2011/nov/27/gothic-fiction-divided-selves> [accessed April 2020].
18. Paterson, 'The Dark Art of Poetry: T.S. Eliot Lecture, 2004'.
19. Paterson, *The Poem: Lyric, Sign, Metre*, 17–18.
20. Paterson, 'Introduction', *New British Poetry*, xxx.
21. Donaghy, 'Wallflowers', *The Shape of the Dance*, 16.
22. Paterson, 'The Dilemma of the Peot [*sic*]', *How Poets Work*, 165.
23. Paterson, *The Poem: Lyric, Sign, Metre*, 670.
24. Paterson, 'The Dilemma of the Peot [*sic*]', *How Poets Work*, 155.

25. Alice Oswald, cited in *The Bloodaxe Book of Poetry Quotations*, ed. Dennis O'Driscoll (Tarset, Northumberland: Bloodaxe Books, 2006), 30.

26. Paterson, 'The Dark Art of Poetry: T.S. Eliot Lecture, 2004'.

27. Edward Larrissy, 'No-Score Drawing: Postmodern Games in Don Paterson', *Don Paterson: Contemporary Critical Essays*, ed. Natalie Pollard (Edinburgh: Edinburgh University Press, 2014), 56.

28. Gilles Deleuze and Félix Guattari, *Kafka: Towards a Minor Literature*, trans. by Dana Polan (Minneapolis, MN: University of Minnesota Press, 1986), 22.

29. Paterson, 'The Dark Art of Poetry: T.S. Eliot Lecture, 2004'.

30. Niall Lucy, *Postmodern Literary Theory* (Oxford: Blackwell Publishers, 1997), 199.

31. O'Brien, 'Don Paterson: *Rain*, Etc', *Poetry Review*, 67.

CHAPTER 5: BREATH, YOU INVISIBLE POEM: *ORPHEUS* (2006)

1. O'Brien, 'Don Paterson: *Rain*, Etc', *Poetry Review*, 69.

2. Rainer Maria Rilke, letter to Countess Margot Sizzo-Noris-Crouy, April 12, 1923, cited in 'Notes' to *Duino Elegies and The Sonnets to Orpheus*, ed. and trans. by Stephen Mitchell (New York: Vintage, 2009), 249.

3. Mark Doty, 'The Singer Sung', *The Guardian* (November 11, 2006), <http://www.theguardian.com/books/2006/nov/11/featuresreviews.guardianreview26> [accessed April 2020].

4. Hugh Haughton, 'Music, Translation and the Patersonnet', *Don Paterson: Contemporary Critical Essays*, 43.

5. Robert Vilain, 'Song is Being', *Times Literary Supplement* (January 19, 2007).

6. Paterson, *101 Sonnets: From Shakespeare to Heaney* (London: Faber, 1999), xv.

7. Ibid., xvi.

8. Ibid.

9. 'Qual è 'l geomètra che tutto s'affige / per misurar lo cerchio, e non ritrova, / pensando, quel principio ond' elli indige, / tal era io a quella vista nova'. Dante, *Paradiso*, Canto XXXIII, ll. 133–5.

10. Stephen Mitchell, 'Notes', in *Duino Elegies* and *The Sonnets to Orpheus*, xix.

11. Rainer Maria Rilke, letter to Lou Andreas-Salomé, June 26, 1914, cited in 'Notes' to *Duino Elegies* and *The Sonnets to Orpheus*, 262.

12. Paterson, *101 Sonnets*, xxvii.

13. Porchia, *Voices*, 47, 61.
14. Rainer Maria Rilke, letter to Katharina Kippenberg, April 2, 1922, cited in 'Notes' to *Duino Elegies* and *The Sonnets to Orpheus*, 265.
15. Rilke, 'Zweiter Teil (Second Part): XIII', *Duino Elegies* and *The Sonnets to Orpheus*, 159.
16. Paterson, 'The Dark Art of Poetry: T.S. Eliot Lecture, 2004'.
17. O'Brien, 'Don Paterson: *Rain*, Etc', *Poetry Review*, 61.
18. Rainer Maria Rilke, letter to Nanny Wunderly-Volkart, July 29, 1920, cited in 'Notes' to *Duino Elegies* and *The Sonnets to Orpheus*, 252.
19. Rilke, 'Erster Teil (First Part): III', *Duino Elegies* and *The Sonnets to Orpheus*, 87.
20. As Paterson argues: 'Song, though, is a uniquely human business. As beautiful as they are – or rather 'as we find them' – whale-song and bird-song are largely concerned with territory and sexual selection, and are barely analogous to the signature twitter of our speech, never mind *Winterreise* or 'Woodstock'. Human song is double: it binds an exclusively human system that we have carefully developed to a universal one, based on physical law, that we have merely learned to manipulate. Fused to music, our speech becomes self-transcending, immediately part of a primal and universal realm in which it can symbolically and literally participate' (*The Poem: Lyric, Sign, Metre*, 6–7). This argument rings philosophically sound, but in its seeming opposition to conventional wisdom and sentiment, it is one that Paterson has perhaps unsurprisingly been moved to defend on a number of occasions, particularly when an earlier version of this statement first appeared in the periodical *Poetry Review*, attracting certain criticisms. 'What I was saying', clarified Paterson, 'is that "song" is music *and* language. The "song" in "birdsong" is a metaphor. Besides, the beauty that we find in the music of birdsong is something we project into it, and to presume that the bird shares our feelings of its charm and expressiveness is an act of horrific anthropocentrism – not the act of empathy or fellow-feeling some folk think it is. None of this makes it any less beautiful, of course' ('Letter to the Editor', *Poetry Review*, 97:4 (Winter 2007/8), 126).
21. Paterson, *The Poem: Lyric, Sign, Metre*, 7–8.
22. Porchia, *Voices*, 25, 51.

CHAPTER 6: NONE OF THIS MATTERS: *RAIN* (2009)

1. A. E. Stallings, 'Poetry for Grown-ups', *Poetry* (May 2010), <http://www.poetryfoundation.org/poetrymagazine/article/239286> [accessed April 2020].
2. Paterson, *The Poem: Lyric, Sign, Metre*, 11.
3. Donaghy, 'Wallflowers', *The Shape of the Dance*, 15–16.
4. O'Brien, 'Don Paterson: *Rain*, Etc', *Poetry Review*, 69.
5. Paterson, *The Poem: Lyric, Sign, Metre*, 108.
6. Ibid.
7. Jan Schreiber, 'Don Paterson's Improbable Distances', *Contemporary Poetry Review* (June 6, 2011), <https://www.cprw.com/don-patersons-improbable-distances> [accessed May 2020].
8. Paterson, 'Night Waves', an interview by Philip Dodd, BBC Radio 4 (October 3, 2012), <http://www.bbc.co.uk/programmes/b01n1s4q> [accessed May 2020].
9. Chiasson, 'Forms of Attention', *The New Yorker*, 116.
10. Paterson, Introduction to *Don't Ask Me What I Mean: Poets in Their Own Words*, eds Clare Brown and Don Paterson (London: Picador, 2003), xi.
11. Chiasson, 116.
12. Paterson, *The Poem: Lyric, Sign, Metre*, 112.
13. Paterson, 'Night Waves', an interview by Philip Dodd, BBC Radio 4.
14. Paterson, *The Poem: Lyric, Sign, Metre*, 111.
15. Ibid., 106.
16. Ibid.
17. Derek Attridge, 'Don Paterson's *Ars Poetica*', *Don Paterson: Contemporary Critical Essays*, 26.
18. Paterson, *The Poem: Lyric, Sign, Metre*, 111.
19. Ibid.
20. Ibid.
21. Ibid., 112.
22. Ibid.
23. A. E. Stallings, 'Poetry for Grown-ups', *Poetry* (May 2010).
24. Chiasson, 116.
25. Adam Newey, 'Review: *Rain* by Don Paterson', *The Guardian* (September 19, 2009), <http://www.guardian.co.uk/books/2009/sep/19/rain-don-paterson-review> [accessed April 2020].
26. Paterson, *The Poem: Lyric, Sign, Metre*, 136.
27. Paterson, 'Frost as a Thinker', a lecture given at the twenty-second Aldeburgh Poetry Festival, November 2010, audio from the Poetry Foundation, <http://www.poetryfoundation.org/features/audioitem/2880> [accessed May 2020].

28. Robert Frost, 'West-Running Brook', *The Poetry of Robert Frost*, ed. Edward Connery Lathem (1971; London: Vintage, 2001), 258.

29. Dai George, 'Degrees of Sight', *Boston Review* (September 9, 2010).

30. Jan Schreiber, 'Don Paterson's Improbable Distances', *Contemporary Poetry Review* (June 6, 2011), <http://www.cprw.com/don-patersons-improbable-distances> [accessed April 2020].

31. Paterson, *The Poem: Lyric, Sign, Metre*, 109.

32. Eliot, 'Hamlet and His Problems', *The Sacred Wood*, 85.

33. Donaghy, 'Wallflowers', *The Shape of the Dance*, 27–8.

34. Newey, 'Review: *Rain* by Don Paterson', *The Guardian*.

35. Paterson, 'Night Waves', an interview by Philip Dodd, BBC Radio 4.

36. Ibid.

37. Ibid.

38. Paterson, *The Poem: Lyric, Sign, Metre*, 336.

CODA

1. O'Brien, 'Don Paterson: *Rain*, Etc', *Poetry Review*, 61.

2. Carol Ann Duffy, cited in 'Best Books of 2009', *The Guardian* (November 28, 2009), <https://www.theguardian.com/books/2009/nov/28/christmas-book-choice-review> [accessed April 2020].

3. Paterson, *The Poem: Lyric, Sign, Metre*, 112.

4. Paterson, 'Night Waves', an interview by Philip Dodd, BBC Radio 4.

5. Paterson, 'The Dark Art of Poetry: T.S. Eliot Lecture, 2004'.

6. Ibid.

7. Paterson, *The Poem: Lyric, Sign, Metre*, 6.

8. Paterson, *101 Sonnets*, xxvii.

9. Ibid., xxv.

10. William Boyd, 'Books of the Year', *New Statesman* (November 21, 2015), <https://www.newstatesman.com/culture/books/2015/11/books-year-essential-ns-reading-list> [accessed April 2020].

11. John Phipps, 'Lamps in Videogames Use Real Electricity', *The London Magazine* (March 31, 2020), <https://www.thelondonmagazine.org/review-zonal-by-don-paterson-if-all-the-world-and-love-were-young-by-stephen-sexton> [accessed April 2020].

12. Paterson, 'The Dilemma of the Peot [*sic*]', *How Poets Work*, 161.

Select Bibliography

Works by Don Paterson

Poetry
Nil Nil (London: Faber, 1993).
God's Gift to Women (London: Faber, 1997).
The Eyes: A Version of Antonio Machado (London: Faber, 1999).
The White Lie: New & Selected Poems (Minneapolis: Graywolf Press, 2001).
Landing Light (London: Faber, 2003; Minneapolis: Graywolf Press, 2004).
Orpheus: A Version of Rilke's Die Sonette an Orpheus (London: Faber, 2006).
Rain (London: Faber, 2009; New York: Farrar, Straus and Giroux, 2010).
Selected Poems (London: Faber, 2012).
40 Sonnets (London: Faber, 2015; New York: Farrar, Straus and Giroux, 2017).
Zonal (London: Faber, 2020).

Prose
The Book of Shadows (London: Picador, 2004).
The Blind Eye: A Book of Late Advice (London: Faber, 2007).
Best Thought, Worst Thought: On Art, Sex, Work and Death (Minneapolis: Graywolf Press, 2008).
Reading Shakespeare's Sonnets: A New Commentary (London: Faber, 2010).
Smith: A Reader's Guide to the Poetry of Michael Donaghy (London: Picador, 2014).
The Poem: Lyric, Sign, Metre (London: Faber, 2018).
The Fall at Home: New and Collected Aphorisms (London: Faber, 2018).

Essays/Lectures
'The Dilemma of the Peot [*sic*]', *How Poets Work*, ed. Tony Curtis (Bridgend, Wales: Seren, 1996), 155–66.
'The Dark Art of Poetry', T. S. Eliot Lecture (October 30, 2004), reproduced in *The Guardian* (November 6, 2004). <https://www.theguardian.com/books/poetry/features/0,12887,1344654,00.html> [accessed May 2020].

'The Lyric Principle', *Poetry Review*, 97:2 and 97:3 (Summer and Autumn 2007), 56–72; 54–70.

'Frost as a Thinker', a lecture given at the twenty-second Aldeburgh Poetry Festival, November 2010. Audio from the Poetry Foundation, <http://www.poetryfoundation.org/features/audioitem/2880> [accessed May 2020].

'The Domain of the Poem', *Poetry Review*, 100:4 and 101:1 (Winter 2010 and Spring 2011), 81–100; 71–95.

Edited Works

Last Words: New Poetry for the New Century, ed. with Jo Shapcott (London: Picador, 1999).

101 Sonnets: From Shakespeare to Heaney (London: Faber, 1999).

Robert Burns: Selected Poems (London: Faber, 2001).

Don't Ask Me What I Mean: Poets in Their Own Words, ed. with Clare Brown (London: Picador, 2003).

New British Poetry, ed. with Charles Simic (Minneapolis: Graywolf Press, 2004).

Train Songs: Poetry of the Railway, ed. with Sean O'Brien (London: Faber, 2013).

The Zoo of the New: Poems to Read Now, ed. with Nick Laird (London: Penguin, 2017).

Critical Studies

Bertram, Vicki, *Gendering Poetry: Contemporary Women and Men Poets* (London: Pandora Press, 2005).

Broom, Sarah, *Contemporary British and Irish Poetry* (Basingstoke: Palgrave MacMillan, 2006).

Corcoran, Neil, ed., *The Cambridge Companion to Twentieth-Century English Poetry* (Cambridge: Cambridge University Press, 2007).

Dósa, Attila, *Beyond Identity: New Horizons in Modern Scottish Poetry* (Amsterdam: Editions Rodopi, 2009).

Fazzini, Marco, ed., *Alba Literaria: A History of Scottish Literature* (Venice: Amos Edizioni, 2005).

Mackay, Peter, Edna Longley, and Fran Brearton, eds, *Modern Irish and Scottish Poetry* (Cambridge: Cambridge University Press, 2011).

McGuire, Matt, and Colin Nicholson, eds, *The Edinburgh Companion to Contemporary Scottish Poetry* (Edinburgh: Edinburgh University Press, 2009).

Parini, Jay, ed., *British Writers: Supplement XVII* (Michigan: Gale-Cengage, 2011).

Pollard, Natalie, *Speaking to You: Contemporary Poetry and Public Address* (Oxford: Oxford University Press, 2012).

——, ed., *Don Paterson: Contemporary Critical Essays* (Edinburgh: Edinburgh University Press, 2014).

Sampson, Fiona, *Beyond the Lyric: A Map of Contemporary British Poetry* (London: Chatto & Windus, 2012).

Schoene, Berthold, ed., *The Edinburgh Companion to Contemporary Scottish Literature* (Edinburgh: Edinburgh University Press, 2007).

Watson, Roderick, *The Literature of Scotland: The Twentieth Century*, 2nd edn (Basingstoke: Palgrave Macmillan, 2007).

Interviews

Blyth, Caroline, 'One All: An Interview with Don Paterson', *Oxford Poetry*, III.3. <http://www.oxfordpoetry.co.uk/texts.php?int=viii3_donpaterson> [accessed May 2020].

Dodd, Philip, 'Night Waves: Don Paterson', BBC Radio 4 (October 3, 2012). <http://www.bbc.co.uk/programmes/b01n1s4q> [accessed May 2020].

Dosa, Attila, 'Don Paterson: The Music of Consciousness', *Beyond Identity: New Horizons in Modern Scottish Poetry* (Amsterdam: Rodopi, 2009), 147–66.

Friel, Raymond, 'Don Paterson, Interviewed', *Talking Verse*, eds Robert Crawford, Henry Hart, David Kinloch, and Richard Price (St Andrews: Verse, 1995), 192–8.

Patterson, Christina, 'Playing the Beautiful Game', *The Independent* (January 9, 2004). <http://www.independent.co.uk/arts-entertainment/books/features/don-paterson-playing-the-beautiful-game-572418.html> [accessed May 2020].

Seaton, Matt, 'It's a Slow Process', *The Guardian* (January 21, 2004). <http://www.guardian.co.uk/books/2004/jan/21/poetry.tseliotprize forpoetry> [accessed May 2020].

Stammers, John, 'Private Enterprise for the Public Good', *Magma*, 12 (Spring 1998), 32–42. <http://poetrymagazines.org.uk/magazine/recordcae4.html?id=3524> [accessed May 2020].

Wareing, Laurence, 'Reading between the Lines', *The Glasgow Herald* (August 30, 2003), 13.

Warner, Ahren, 'I Think Clarity is the Way to Go', *Poetry London*, 74 (Spring 2013), 35–8.

Wroe, Nicholas, 'Leading Light', *The Guardian* (November 25, 2006). <http://www.guardian.co.uk/books/2006/nov/25/featuresreviews.guardianreview7> [accessed May 2020].

Useful Websites

Paterson's official website is located at: http://donpaterson.net/ Includes biographical and bibliographical information, plus assorted links to other online material.

The Scottish Poetry Library holds an extensive digital entry on Paterson: https://www.scottishpoetrylibrary.org.uk/poet/don-paterson/ Includes a number of poems from across Paterson's oeuvre to date, freely available to read.

A manuscript collection of notebooks and papers is held by the National Library of Scotland (July 2007). Acc. 12689. Inventory can be found at: http://www.nls.uk/catalogues/online/cnmi/inventories/acc12689.pdf

Index